To Jason
with very best
wishes
Len freller

The Gift of Life

Leon Schaller's Story

Malcolm, Clive and Linda Schaller

The Gift of Life

Leon Schaller's Story

Ann Rosen

Quill in association with THE HOLOCAUST CENTRE

The Gift of Life

Leon Schaller's Story

Ann Rosen

Published in Great Britain by
Quill Press in association with The Holocaust Centre
The Hub,
Haskell House,
152 West End Lane
London.
NW6 1SD

British Library Catalogue in Publication Data
A catalogue record for this book is available from the British Library.

ISBN 978-0-9555009-5-4

Design and artwork, Glen Powell Graphic Design
Printed and bound by Good News Digital Books

Cover Photograph: Leon Schaller as a child

CONTENTS

To the memory of

the hundreds of relatives and school friends who perished in the Holocaust,
my devoted parents, Chana and Berl Schaller, who left Germany just in time,
and my beloved wife, Freda, the inspiration behind my success.

FOREWORD

At one of the supreme moments of the Jewish year, during the Ten Days of Repentance, we say a prayer: "Write us in the book of life." When Jews think of life, they think of a book.

That book – the book of Jewish life – is the oldest and most remarkable in the history of civilization. It extends back four thousand years. It tells the story of a tempestuous love affair between one small yet vivid people and God. Every generation has added a chapter; and the locations of the drama have covered every land under the sun and almost every circumstance from tragedy to triumph.

The good and great Jewish lives in any generation are part of that story, and Leon Schaller's is one. He is one of that small band of people without whose generosity and wise counsel British Jewry's, as well as Israel's, religious, social, medical and educational activities would be greatly reduced. Leon has understood at every level of his being that, Jewishly, to live is to give.

Leon is a man I love and admire. He and his beloved wife Freda of blessed memory created a marriage, a home and a family that were a source of blessing to all whose lives they touched. For 60 years to see them together was to see two lives intertwined in *chein*, *chessed* and *rachamim*, grace, kindness and compassion, and it was lovely to witness.

Leon's beginnings were not easy. He had to work hard for everything he achieved. But he knew that the success with which God had blessed him was not for him alone, but so that he could bring blessing into other lives. Together he and Freda epitomised the Jewish values of *tzedakah*, *gemillut chesed* and love of fellow humans. They did good on a vast scale, and did so quietly, unostentatiously, and with true humility.

To read the story of such a life is to be lifted, and to have one's sense of possibility enlarged. The best way of knowing what can be done in a single lifetime is to read such stories, for they take us beyond theory and abstraction and show us living examples of moral greatness, which I define as the defeat of probability by the power of possibility.

May you, like me, be inspired by Leon's story. May God continue to bless him and may he continue to bless us.

Jonathan Sacks

Chief Rabbi Lord Sacks
Ellul 5770

ACKNOWLEDGEMENTS

The idea of *The Gift of Life* came from a conversation with Dr Aron Balkin, a close friend and colleague of Malcolm Schaller. I met Aron at a barmitzvah in the summer of 2007. He knew that Leon Schaller had a story that had to be told and kindly introduced me to Malcolm. Two years later, I had the pleasure of meeting the whole Schaller family at the dedication in Ilford of the Bet Midrash in memory of Freda (z'l).

I am very grateful for the helpful input provided by all members of the Schaller family; for the warm tributes and messages from family and friends; and to the Chief Rabbi, Lord Sacks, for his moving Foreword.

I have been fortunate to have the support of Dr Wendy Whitworth, my patient and meticulous editor, and of Glen Powell, a talented and artistic designer. Thanks are also due to the United States Holocaust Memorial Museum, Washington, for the use of photographs and archive material.

Lastly, it has been a great privilege – and a lot of fun – to work with Leon. I have been constantly amazed by the scale and range of his involvement and generosity to so many causes and individuals. Writing his story has been – and will continue to be – an inspiration.

Ann Rosen
December 2010

INTRODUCTION

On 6 November 1938, Herschel Grynszpan, a young Jewish man, walked into the German Embassy in Paris and shot Ernst vom Rath, a German diplomat. Vom Rath died of his wound three days later.

Despite overwhelming evidence that the Nazis had been planning the widescale destruction of European Jewry for some time, the attack on vom Rath by a 17-year-old Jew was used by Germany to demonstrate the fact that the Jews were the enemy. In reality, Grynszpan's act was one of defiance in protest against the terrible treatment afforded to Polish Jews – and among them his own parents. Along with 12,000 Jews of Polish descent who had been living in Germany, they had been expelled from Germany and sent to Poland.

Grynszpan's dramatic act of defiance reflected his desire for the world to know of the fate the Jews were suffering. He knew that in committing this assassination, his own life would effectively be over. After his arrest, a postcard adressed to his parents was found that he had obviously hoped would be forwarded to them. His words clearly express his desperation:

With G-d's help, I could not do otherwise, may G-d forgive me, the heart bleeds when I hear of your tragedy and that of the 12,000 Jews. I must protest so that the whole world hears my protest, and that I will do.

Forgive me.

Grynszpan's act is remembered by Jewish historians as the first demonstration of opposition to Nazi oppression. To the Germans of the time, it was used as a clear proof that the Jews were the agents of their own misfortune...

When the news of vom Rath's death reached Hitler, the following instruction was given through Goebbels, his propaganda minister:

The Führer has decided that demonstrations should not be prepared or organised by the Party, but insofar as they erupt spontaneously, they are not to be hampered.

Within hours of the death of vom Rath, the Nazis launched a massive pogrom against Jews throughout Germany. *Kristallnacht*, the Night of the Broken Glass, will be remembered as the night that the Holocaust began.

On the night of 9-10 November 1938, German civilians throughout the country, armed with sledgehammers and axes, went to work on the destruction of Jewish property and businesses. At the end of this 'spontaneous' uprising, the destruction of about 200 synagogues had occurred and 7,000 Jewish shops had been destroyed. Throughout Germany, fires burning sacred books and Torah scrolls blazed through the night. Over 30,000 Jews were arrested and taken to concentration camps. In neighbouring Austria, similar events occurred. Austrian citizens attacked their neighbours and colleagues – people with whom they had previously lived and worked harmoniously. After *Kristallnacht*, official reports in Austria stated that 191 synagogues had been destroyed and 100,000 Jews arrested.

An English journalist who witnessed the event described:

Fashionably dressed women clapping their hands and screaming with glee, while respectable middle-class mothers held up their babies to see the fun.

I will never forget *Kristallnacht* – the sounds I heard and the sights I saw in Cologne that night are impossible to forget. It began with the clatter of general commotion, and then we heard lots of noise and people shouting. Although we were inside our apartment, we could hear the crowd chanting, *"Juden Raus!"* ("Jews out!") My cousin Adele was staying with us at the time and we were both curious and ran out to see what was happening. I am sure my parents would have urged us to stay indoors, but somehow, despite this we went out onto the streets. There were two main streets and all along them the shop windows had been smashed. Our apartment was nearby. We then went down the Hohestrasse, the shopping street where the fine Jewish shops were, and they too had all been wrecked. We watched in horror and disbelief as we saw respectable-looking people smashing the shop fronts and helping themselves to whatever they wanted. We saw looting going on all over town and nobody did anything about it. The Nazis were everywhere overseeing the whole operation and it seemed that all the normal rules of behaviour had been abandoned on that night.

I don't know what made us run to the Roonstrasse, where our synagogue was. This majestic building was the pride of our community and the focal point of our religious life. When we got there, we saw that it had been set alight. Crowds had gathered round to watch the spectacle. The building was not yet totally destroyed when firemen began to hose down the building. I think there was talk of the fire spreading to the neighbouring buildings, so the fire was put out. As I remember it, the lower levels and the side of the building were destroyed, but the frontage and upper floors remained. I don't think we spoke about what we were witnessing. It was so unbelievable; we were just stunned. Terrified, we ran back to our apartment and locked the doors. It was only later that we learnt that the synagogue had not been empty – the caretaker had been inside and was burnt alive.

Fortunately, we only witnessed a small part of the devastation that took place that night and our fear meant that we did not stay out for very long. There was another magnificent synagogue, the Glockengasse in the centre of Cologne. We would go there occasionally for *Shabbat*. It had been built in 1861 and was an incredible Moorish-style building with minarets and stained-glass windows. Services there were strictly Orthodox. This synagogue was led by Rabbi Joseph Hirsch Dunner, who managed to escape the Nazis with his wife and child. Subsequently, Rabbi Dunner became a prominent and influential rabbi in the Orthodox community of Stamford Hill. The Glockengasse was burnt to the ground on that night. Today, the Cologne Opera House occupies the spot where Rabbi Dunner's community once worshipped. All that remains there now is a plaque in memory of that once flourishing community.

I was only 16 years old at the time, just a year younger than Herschel Grynszpan, and unlike him I was not yet politically aware. I was unsure how to interpret the events I had witnessed and looked to my parents for guidance. I don't think my parents felt really worried about our physical safety until *Kristallnacht*.

Reading about Herschel Grynszpan now, so many years after those horrific events, it is strange to reflect on the similarities between our lives. Many Jews of Polish origin, like Grynszpan's parents and mine, had moved from Poland to make a new life in Germany. Ironically, this was because they had wanted to give their families a better standard of living. Although we had lived in different towns – he was in Hanover, I was in Cologne – our childhood experiences were likely to have been similar. We both went to Jewish sports clubs, came from loving families and lived in close-knit Jewish communities.

But now the security of our lives, and that of our families, was being torn away from us. Although it is difficult for me to recall many of the precise events from that terrible time, the feelings and emotions from then are unforgettable. Fear and anxiety dominated my life. When I was not in the comfort of our home, I was constantly watchful. I also remember a feeling of total helplessness; even my parents did not know what to do. If we looked to our communal leaders for advice, we received no clear direction, as they too felt powerless.

It is hard to describe the sense of confusion and betrayal that I felt as a young boy at the time. What is a child to understand when he sees respectable adults looting Jewish department stores and the local police simply standing by? I remember that my parents talked about our neighbours in the apartment block, who had been friendly with us. They were very left-wing politically and had said they opposed the Nazis. But on *Kristallnacht*, some of them were seen to be looting the Jewish shops with the rest of the crowd.

Kristallnacht was very much the turning point for me, although we had experienced antisemitism for years but had not really wanted to believe how bad the situation was. I must have been about 12 when I had my first personal taste of it; it was so unpleasant and shocking that I still remember it today. One day, the barber who had been cutting my hair since I was a tiny child simply refused to serve me. He said it was against the law to cut my hair. I wondered about the thoughts that were in this man's head – did he really think a young boy posed a threat to the Reich?

On *Kristallnacht*, similar events were played out thousands of times in towns all over Europe. We had suddenly become non-people. How were we to survive? Where would we go and who would take us?

Like millions of other Jews all over Europe, these were the questions that my parents faced. They did not know where to go and they were unsure of what to do. They only knew of life in Romania, Poland and Germany. They had not travelled widely and had little experience of life outside their community. They knew that they were no longer safe in Germany and had to make a decision about our future. But at that stage, nobody could envisage the scale of destruction that was to befall our people.

Over 70 years have passed since the terrible events that caused the destruction of European Jewry. My children have asked me to tell the story of my early years for their sake and for future generations.

Since I was among the few fortunate ones and finally feel able to share my memories of that sad chapter in our history, I will try to record as much as I can recall of those years. Perhaps those who read this will learn something that will help to shape a better future for generations to come.

I came from a large and thriving family; both my parents had many siblings and spoke warmly of their wider families. My mother, Chana, (née Freibrun), came from Stanislawow, Poland. My father, Berl Schaller, came from Babin, Romania. But beyond this, I do not even know precisely how many relatives I had. Despite my parents' hopes, I know that no family members came to find us after the war.

My grandparents, aunts and uncles perished in Poland and in the Ukraine. Like millions of others, nothing of them remains. Their homes and villages were wiped out. For them, we have no graves and no memorials – all that we have is the knowledge that they once lived. My main hope is that by recording this incomplete testimony, those who perished will not be forgotten. May their memory be blessed.

Photo from the Freibrun family album, c. 1920

The Freibrun family in Poland, early 1930s

Family photos from the 1930s: Chana's siblings in Stanislawow, Poland

From the family album: thought to be my grandmother holding my mother as a baby

Beginnings

Although I was born in Cologne, my generation was the first and last German generation in our family. My parents' roots and those of their ancestors were all in Eastern Europe. The world from which they came was one that was rarely discussed and about which I know very little. In those days, we did not travel much and once people moved to a new country, there was limited communication between family members. I do not remember ever meeting any of my grandparents or knowing family members who lived in countries other than Germany. For this reason, I can only give a very incomplete history of my family.

Both of my parents came from different parts of Eastern Europe; and both were born in regions that changed hands and political regimes frequently. Even the names of the villages about which they spoke no longer exist today.

Stanislawow in Poland had been the home of my mother's family, the Freibruns, for generations. It is now known as Ivano-Frankivsk, a historic city located in south-western Ukraine. This area had a complex history and had been part of the Polish empire, the Austro-Hungarian empire and the Russian empire in the eighteenth and nineteenth centuries. Jews had lived in this region for centuries and at times they had played a prominent role in civic affairs and cultural life. Clearly, there was a thriving Jewish community in this area which grew significantly during the 1930s. According to the Polish census of 1931, there were 26,996 Jews within the area; by 1941, there were said to be approximately 40,000.

My father came from a small place called Babin, close to Czernowitz. Today this region is part of Ukraine, but in my father's time, it was part of Romania and my father had done national service in the Austro-Hungarian Army.

I was born on 15 August 1922 in Cologne, Germany, and called Leo. My Hebrew name was Eliezer after my maternal grandfather, Eliezer Freibrun, who must have died sometime before my birth. Everyone at home and at school called me Leo. It is interesting that my parents chose German names for us, so that we fitted in with the environment in which we lived. My parents still used their Jewish names among family and friends. I was the youngest of three children; the eldest was my sister Regina (1915-2003), and

Berl Schaller in Austro-Hungarian Army uniform

then my brother Hermann, who now lives in Monte Carlo, was born in 1917. My mother's name was Chana/ Anna (1895-1976) and my father's Berl/ Bernard (1890-1976).

The Nazis' mission to annihilate all traces of Jewish life was entirely successful in the parts of Ukraine/ Poland/ Romania from which my grandparents came. For this reason, I know very little about the families they came from and the lives my parents lived before they moved to Germany.

✡ ✡ ✡

My father with my brother Hermann (left) and me, 1930

With my class, 1932. I am in the third row from the front, fourth right, wearing a cap.

EARLY YEARS

Cologne, a beautiful cathedral city on the banks of the River Rhine. The cultural centre of the Rhineland, it boasts museums and theatres. It is one of the oldest cities in Germany and its history dates back to Roman times. Its university is among the oldest in Europe. Since it is situated in the western part of Germany, it is close to Holland, Belgium and France.

I do not know precisely why my parents had both decided individually to move to the city of Cologne. It was definitely primarily a decision to ease the financial burdens on their parents and achieve a better standard of living. At the time, there was a large community of Jews from Poland in Cologne and it is likely that they were following the movement of friends and people in similar circumstances.

My mother's decision to move from Poland would have been influenced by the fact that her older sister, Ronchi Winterfeld, had moved to Aachen with her husband. Initially, she might possibly have lived with Ronchi in Aachen, which was only 60 kilometres from Cologne.

My uncle, Chaim Winterfeld, was a successful businessman and throughout my childhood, the Winterfelds were the only relatives we knew. There were nine Winterfeld children: Adele, Clara, Minna, Sara, Johanna, Rosa, Max, Morritz and Jacob. I really enjoyed the company of my cousins and our families were very close.

Both of my parents had grown up in *shtetls* in Eastern Europe. Coming from large families where money and educational opportunities were scarce, they had hoped to provide us with a wider range of options than they had experienced in their childhood.

For each of them, moving to Germany was to be a new start. It was a progressive move away from the rural village life of their families. Germany was far more industrialised and technologically advanced than the rural villages that they had known. My father, who was a metallurgist, easily found work in Cologne and was able to send money back to his family in Romania.

I don't know how my parents met, nor do I remember them talking about their courtship and wedding to us. But there was a large community of Jews from Eastern Europe living in Cologne at the time. Traditionally, it was expected that young men and women were introduced to each other by relatives or older members of the community. *Shidduchim* – marriage introductions – were very much the norm in their society and I imagine that their marriage was the result of a *shidduch*.

It is easy to understand my parents' decision to choose this city as the place to set up their first home. It must have seemed like the perfect place for them to begin life as a married couple and raise a family.

In the early 1930s, when I was a very young child, they were happy to take advantage of all that Cologne offered. We were also able to travel in Europe and I have happy memories of family outings to leisure parks in Holland. In my early childhood, I enjoyed seaside holidays in Knokke, Belgium, and we stayed in the Jewish hotel there.

For a child growing up in Cologne, the city had everything. There were plenty of parks and green spaces in which to play. There were

Jewish schools and clubs. My parents saw themselves as slightly more enlightened and modern than the previous generation. Although my upbringing was not as intensely religious as that of my parents, they had definite plans and aspirations for us. They hoped to give us a traditionally Jewish upbringing in which we celebrated all the major festivals and always had a traditional *Shabbat*.

At that time, there were about 15,000 Jews living in Cologne and we were very much part of a thriving community. The neighbourhood in which we lived was predominantly Jewish and our friends were all Jews of Polish origin. As I remember it, about 80 per cent of our neighbours were Jewish, as were most of the people in our apartment building. But we were also on friendly terms with the non-Jewish neighbours who lived nearby. All my closest friends lived in our building.

Our home was a happy one and I can still picture our apartment in Cologne. We lived in an apartment block with all the modern facilities of the time. Our flat was on the third floor in a four-storey building that accommodated eight families. We had three bedrooms, a bathroom and a separate toilet. When we were young, I shared my bedroom with my older brother, Hermann. My brother left home when he was about 16 and went to work for my uncle Chaim Winterfeld in Aachen. Uncle Chaim owned a clothes shop and my parents were happy that Hermann was given the opportunity to work in the business.

In those days, we walked everywhere as a crowd of friends. A whole group of us would go to school in the mornings together. There were a few local shops that were our favourite haunts. In particular, I remember the bakery where we would stop and buy a delicious poppy-seed-covered roll on the way to school. We also used to buy sweets at a shop called Tietz, a large store that was owned by a Jewish family.

My school, the *Israelitische Volkschule*, was about 15 minutes' walk away. This was a Jewish primary school and I attended there from about the age of six. There were separate classes for boys and girls. There were about 30 boys in my class. We had very strict German disciplinarian teachers. As far as I can remember, I was a very well-behaved little boy. Although my teacher, Mr Jacoby, used the cane when necessary, I don't remember it ever being used on me!

My favourite subject at school was Geography. I enjoyed learning about other countries and was interested to know about the oceans and mountains. I had a globe at home and used to enjoy looking at all the faraway countries that I imagined I might visit sometime in the future.

The happiest times I remember are of playing football with my friends in the school yard. In the holidays, my mother would go and visit her sister, Ronchi Winterfeld, in the town of Aachen. During that time, I would sometimes be left alone in the care of my father. This was something I absolutely loved. He worked as a metallurgist and would sometimes take me to see where he worked. I really enjoyed seeing the huge vats of different metals being sorted and melted

On holiday in Bad Aachen, c. 1934

18

down. I felt a great sense of prestige at being allowed to be with my father at his workplace. In those days, children were very much kept separate from the adults.

We lived on the edge of a working-class area and were considered a bit better off than most of our neighbours. As far as I remember, we always had enough food and in my childhood, I never felt anything was lacking. This was not the case for some of our friends, who received welfare food packages and assistance from the community *Gemeinde*. My father was a kind and charitable man who was always helping people in the neighbourhood. He was extremely good with his hands and would fix things for people. I remember that he always did some of the more difficult domestic jobs at home for my mother. For example, every morning he would be up early in order to clear out the ash from the stove.

The kitchen was dominated by a large coal-burning stove which was used to heat the apartment and also to heat food. There was a strong smell in the apartment from the paraffin heaters. In those days, we did not have a fridge, but a cold-storage system that might seem somewhat antiquated today! Ice was delivered to us several times a week. It was then placed in a huge bucket at the base of the 'ice cupboard'. This cold-storage arrangement had several shelves onto which food was placed and the door comprised a large metal grid.

My mother was the embodiment of the traditional Jewish mother – a warm and loving person. She was dedicated to every aspect of caring for her family and was busy every day running the house. She was a very cheerful person who loved music; she was always singing when she went about her daily chores. I remember her singing both Jewish melodies and popular German songs.

My parents were very happy together and were very much a partnership. They were both hard-working – if my mother was busy running around, my father would always tell her to sit down and relax and he would help her with the chores. But I do remember that there was one constant source of conflict – my father liked to keep the apartment warm and my mother liked fresh air and open windows. They would often argue about this.

Every day, my mother would shop for bread and milk locally, and when I was a young boy, I always went with her. She knew everyone in our neighbourhood and would often stop and chat with all the neighbours. There were also extensive preparations for *Shabbat*, which was always the highlight of the week, and these preparations took several days. They involved going to the market to buy chicken and carp and then preparing these delicacies.

Shabbat was very much a day spent in the company of family and friends. On Friday night, I would accompany my father to the *Steibl*, a small prayer house that was next door to our house. This was convenient and many of my friends from the neighbourhood joined us there. Every Friday night, my mother would prepare a feast. This began with *Kiddush*, the traditional blessing over wine, and the welcoming in of the *Shabbat*. We would then have mother's home-baked *challot*, *Shabbat* bread. The meal would consist of a starter of stuffed carp, followed by chicken soup with *lockshen*. The main course would be cooked chicken accompanied by *tzimmes*, glazed carrots. I was always amazed by my mother's ability to prepare such an incredible spread on such limited resources.

On *Shabbat* morning, we would go to the Roonstrasse, a grand, formal synagogue that was about 15 minutes' walk from our house. After the service, it would be my job to collect the lunch from the communal oven at the local baker's. This was a stew with meat and beans known as *chollent*.

The bakery shop was a focal point of communal life. It had a large oven that was used by the entire community. My mother also used to make her own *challot* and every Friday I would have to take them there to be baked in the communal oven.

During *Shabbat* the bakery oven was left burning through the night. Since we were not allowed to light a flame or cook on the Sabbath, this communal facility ensured that we had hot food on *Shabbat* morning.

After *Shabbat* lunch, I would be free to play and I would always meet up with my friends from the apartment block at the nearby *Volksgarten*, the local park. My closest friend was Fredi Hofrichter, who lived in my block. A group of us would meet up and just spend the afternoon together.

When I was not left in my father's care during the long summer months, I was sent to a Jewish youth camp not far from Cologne, in Bad Kreuznach, a spa town which is on a tributary of the Rhine. It was in the countryside and gave me the opportunity to play with other children. We did play acting and played table tennis. We went for outings in the forest with other Jewish children from all over the Rhineland. I remember that when my parents suggested that I go there, I was very worried about being separated from them, but after my initial worries, and having been given some money to spend, I really enjoyed those camps. I loved being in the beautiful countryside and my parents encouraged me to go there.

My mother made several trips back to Poland during those years to visit her family in Stanislawow. I think she had a great sense of loyalty to them and would help them financially. Neither my father, nor any of us children, would accompany her on these visits, so we never really knew about the life she had left behind, nor did we hear much about her relatives. She was a prolific letter writer and would correspond with her family regularly, but sadly we do not have any letters from that time.

The rebuilt Roonstrasse Synagogue, Cologne

BARMITZVAH

In the summer of 1935, I celebrated my barmitzvah, the ceremony that marks the beginning of the transition to adulthood. From the age of 13, a Jewish male is obliged to keep all the *mitzvot*, commandments, and from a Jewish perspective is no longer a child.

Since we had no family in Cologne, my parents chose to celebrate this rite of passage with my cousins, the Winterfelds, in Aachen. My uncle Chaim was a warden in the synagogue and very active in communal affairs there. I had nine first cousins in Aachen, to whom I felt very close, and I loved being part of this large, warm, extended family.

At the time, Aachen had a large and wealthy Jewish population. There was the *Judenplatz*, the Jewish square, which was dominated by the Old Synagogue. This was an impressive building that had been built in 1862. It represented the status and success of the community in Aachen and was the favoured place of worship of the more assimilated German Jews. They were Germans of the Jewish persuasion.

The *Judenplatz* comprised several buildings, all for the use of the Jewish community. They were used by the *cheder*, local Hebrew classes. There were also the clubs, such as *Habonim* and *Hechalutz*. These were the Zionist youth groups that were gaining popularity among my friends as they felt the tide of antisemitism was rising.

We were *Ostjuden*, Jews from Poland, who at that time were more strongly religious. We would not pray in the grand central synagogue, but worshipped in a smaller adjoining building, which was less imposing and where the organ was not played on *Shabbat*.

I do not recall many of the guests who attended the service that day, but my friend Issy Hausmann, who lived in Aachen at the time, remembers being a guest there and recalls that I read my Torah portion very well! He recalls a lovely festive atmosphere and a *Kiddush*, reception, after the service on *Shabbat* morning.

I am sure that like most barmitzvah boys, I was not fully aware of the tremendous significance of this event. For my family, it may well have been the last family *simcha* (celebration) in Germany.

Just over three years after my barmitzvah, on *Kristallnacht*, 9-10 November 1938, the Nazis set the old synagogue alight. They did not bother to destroy our modest synagogue. Once the Nazis had destroyed the grand building at the centre of the Jewish square, the community of Aachen understood their intention to obliterate all forms of Jewish life from this once prosperous town.

The Old Synagogue, Aachen

The Old Synagogue, Aachen, after
Kristallnacht

The Nazis invade the Rhineland, 1936
©USHMM

THE BEGINNING OF THE END
(1933-1938)

Every year in Cologne, at 11 minutes past 11 on the 11th of the 11th month, the annual carnival is held. This is the highlight of the year for children living in Cologne. The first carnival was held there in 1823 and the tradition has continued until today.

As children, we felt very patriotic towards Germany and proud to be part of the carnival procession. For us, it was an incredibly exciting occasion. I remember that my father always hired a horse and carriage for this event; we all dressed in disguise and went round the town admiring all the colourful floats and displays. I am not sure in which year our participation in this annual highlight came to an end. We certainly would have participated in 1932, when I was ten years old. But by 1935, the climate had turned rather ugly and the carnival – which had been an occasion that united all the residents of the city – reflected this. The 1935 floats at the carnival were used to display antisemitic messages and racist symbols adorned the displays. Of course, at the time, I was unaware of the sinister message the Nazis were spreading, nor did I have any inkling of how successful their propaganda would be. For me, it was just another aspect of life that had once been enjoyable, but from which I was now excluded.

So whenever I try to remember my childhood, I feel an overwhelming sense of sadness. The dark cloud that the Nazis brought to Europe hung heavily over my life from my earliest years.

I was only a boy of ten when, in 1933, Hitler came to power. I don't think I knew anything about the specifics of what was happening in Europe. I was a child and was kept as one. I clearly remember that I was often sent to play when the adults were deep in serious conversation. They made sure to protect me from what was happening – my parents spoke to each other in Yiddish or Polish and, despite my best efforts, I was unable to understand either of these languages.

But although I might not have understood their conversations, I felt their mood and read their expressions. I was a sensitive child and from 1933, everything in our lives was to change. For me, there was a sharp division between the security of our home, the environment that my parents created around me and the world outside, which was becoming increasingly threatening to our lives.

The Nazis were very thorough in their approach and studied the demographics and population of each town before implementing their plan to enforce control. The Rhineland was an important area to conquer and within it, Cologne was the largest and most important city, both industrially and culturally.

From the outset, the Nazis were very keen to make their presence felt in Cologne. It was a town of great strategic and military importance, being so close to France, Holland and Belgium. They were unsure how easy it would be to win support among the citizens of Cologne because the population was very mixed and there were many communists and Catholics living in the city. These groups were not traditionally thought to be associated with Nazi ideology. However, with a subtle blend of propaganda and 'education', Nazi ideology filtered through to the population of Cologne as effectively as it had done in other parts of Germany.

In 1933, the Nazi boycott of Jewish shops was enforced throughout Germany. It began on 1 April 1933 when Storm Troops appeared outside Jewish shops with placards saying, "Germans, do not enter!" This boycott of Jewish businesses gained momentum and was just as effective in Cologne as elsewhere. In all major cities, German Jews who had been loyal German citizens and served in the German Army, found their businesses being boycotted by their neighbours.

In April 1933, the Nazis began to implement laws that banned non-Aryans from working within Germany. The Party propaganda declared the impossibility of being both Jewish and German. If you were Jewish, you were by definition an enemy of the German state and consequently had to be weeded out. In towns all over Germany, there was competition as to who could implement the new law most thoroughly. In Berlin, they began with 'retiring' Jewish servants and this was followed swiftly by the dismissal of Jewish doctors and academics. In many towns, Jewish professionals were arrested and imprisoned. Opponents of the regime, often along with innocent bystanders, were beaten at random. Jews were openly beaten in the streets and a few were shot as the Jewish population was gradually terrorised.

An organised policy of public book-burnings followed. In May 1933, 34 staged public book-burning ceremonies took place. All books with any Jewish connection were to be destroyed. This included the publications of all the great Jewish writers whose work had previously been respected internationally. The works of Karl Marx, Bertolt Brecht and Ernest Hemingway and those of hundreds of scientists and academics were all incinerated.

On 10 May 1933, a huge bonfire was built outside the Berlin opera house. This was a major national event and thousands of civilians came to participate while Goebbels, the Minister of Propaganda, made a keynote speech, declaring:

> *My fellow students, German men and women, the era of exaggerated Jewish intellectualism is now at an end. The triumph of the German revolution has cleared a path for the German way; and the future German man will not just be a man of books, but also a man of character and it is to this end that we want to educate you.*

In dozens of towns throughout the country, similar events occurred. At the ancient university of Cologne, students set up a huge makeshift amphitheatre to ensure maximum participation.

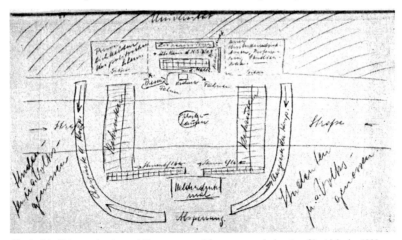

Sketch of the Cologne university amphitheatre constructed for spectators at the burning of Jewish books, 1933
© *USHMM*

Among the 25,000 books burnt at that time was the work of the esteemed German poet Heinrich Heine, who was born Jewish, but had been baptised. Heine had been a sharp critic and observer of German society. Almost a century before the Nazis came to power, he had made the strange prophecy:

Wherever books will be burned, men also in the end will burn.

The Jewish population of Germany was unsure how to react to this widespread violence. A significant proportion chose to leave; between 1933 and 1934, 50,000 Jews left Germany out of a total population of 500,000. In the early days, emigration was actively encouraged.

Most Jews, however, remained in Germany. They had been living a settled life there for centuries, felt a loyalty to Germany and were rooted in the past. Thousands had fought for Germany in the First World War. To them, the dismissal of the brightest academics and those who had contributed so much to building up German culture made no sense and must simply be a temporary crisis.

For a long time, my parents felt they had no option but to remain where they were. They had not lived in Cologne for very long and did not have anywhere to go. Also, they were in a relatively fortunate position compared to many. My father worked for a Jewish-owned company, so he was employed throughout the 1930s. Although Jews were suffering all around us, we were not directly feeling all the effects of the viciously antisemitic laws. Like the vast majority of Jews in Germany who did not expect the violence to last, perhaps my parents waited, hoping the antisemitism would pass.

If Jews within Germany thought that the period of antisemitism was simply a passing phase, the implementation of the Nuremberg

Laws on 15 September 1935 was an indication that the Nazis' determination to persecute Jews was to be on an unprecedented scale. These laws meant that Jews no longer had any rights of citizenship. Having suffered major discrimination for the previous three years, the Jews were now deprived of most of their remaining rights. After the Nuremberg Laws, German policy became very clear. As a visiting British official reported, "The Jew is to be eliminated and the state has no regard for the manner of the elimination."

As the effect of anti-Jewish laws spread throughout Germany, Jews were forced to hand over their businesses into Aryan hands. The Nazis sent representatives to other European countries to help spread anti-Jewish sentiment. Anti-Jewish riots broke out in Romania, Ukraine and Poland in 1936. So if my parents had ever entertained thoughts of returning to the countries of their birth, where their families still lived, the situation in those parts of Eastern Europe was just as bad as in Germany.

As well as intensifying his war against the Jews, Hitler was also expanding his military programme. On 7 March 1936, he began to re-arm the Rhineland. This area had been demilitarised under the terms of the Treaty of Versailles, the international agreement signed by all the major powers at the end of the First World War.

This was a blatant violation of the treaty and Hitler's first success at breaking international law. Since neither Britain nor France did anything actively to challenge the German action, Hitler interpreted this as an indication that he could do what he wanted.

In a strange way, it might have been fortunate for us that we were living in Cologne. In 1936, when we saw the Brownshirts march through the town, we were made very aware of the power of the German Army. Had we lived in another town, we would not have witnessed the same display of military defiance. It was a very strong warning to the Jews of Cologne. The re-arming of the Rhineland was a deliberate show of strength by the Nazis and the combination of their military power and ruthless antisemitic policies must have left my parents in no doubt as to the dangers of the situation in which they found themselves.

In 1937, the swastika flew from many buildings in Cologne, including the cathedral, so the Nazis need not have been concerned about gaining the cooperation of the city's Catholic population.

✡ ✡ ✡

The swastika flying over Cologne Cathedral, 1937
© *USHMM*

A Minority within a Minority

Before Hitler came to power, we were as free to enjoy our lives as other German citizens. Gradually, though, during the 1930s, the things we were able to do and the places we were allowed to visit became fewer and fewer. I only remember all this vaguely and from a child's perspective. I did not understand why suddenly we could not go to public swimming pools or visit certain places. As a child, I was aware that this felt bad for me personally. I am not sure that I understood that Jews were gradually being excluded from all aspects of life in Germany.

I don't remember exactly when my formal schooling came to an end, but there was a gradual feeling that our world was contracting. I was aware that teachers were leaving the school and not being replaced. Children were also leaving because they were emigrating to other countries. I was at the Jewish primary school, the *Israelitische Volkschule*, but did not attend secondary school after that.

My memory of my education after the *Volkschule* is not clear. The school I would have attended after this was the Yavne School, but that never happened. I know that the Jewish community was very active in setting up welfare organisations, and among these a trade school was established. Since Jewish young people were banned from attending colleges and were not going to receive apprenticeships, the community had to become totally self-sufficient. In order to give us expertise with which to earn a living, we were taught skills such as carpentry and locksmithing. I am not sure what the thinking was behind this training, since after 1935 the law did not allow ordinary Germans to employ us. At the same time, the community was becoming increasingly impoverished, so our chances of finding work within Germany were declining. Perhaps it was hoped that if we had skills, it would be easier for us to have something to offer when we were able to emigrate. By all accounts, the situation in Cologne was becoming more desperate for Jews who remained there. By 1936, thousands of people were dependent on communal help for their basic necessities.

When we were out in the streets, we were always fearful. I remember hearing the story of a young child who had said something disparaging to some Nazi soldiers in the street and had never been seen again. I heard my parents saying that a jar containing this child's ashes was brought back to the parents. Stories like this were so unbelievable, I am not sure if we thought they were true. We knew not to talk to the Nazis and not to say anything that might be heard by them. We were afraid to go anywhere on our own and always went out in groups; and whenever we were out in the streets, we always rushed home to the safety of our apartment.

Despite the fact that the only language I knew was German, and the only place I had lived in was Cologne, the German Jews who had lived in Germany for centuries never quite considered us as part of their community. It is well known that the Jewish population were among the most patriotic and loyal German citizens. Consequently,

they looked down on those who came from Poland and called them
'*Polacken*'.

Occasionally, street fights would break out between the children
whose families had been in Germany for generations and children like
us whose parents were refugees. My childhood friend from Aachen,
Issy Hausmann, who is a few years older than me and now lives in Tel
Aviv, remembers that I was a strong fighter and a defender of any of
my crowd who were started on by older boys.

These skirmishes were not very serious and although we might have
had scuffles in the street with different groups, these divisions did not go
very deep. We were together in the Jewish youth clubs, where many of
the young people recognised that all Jews had a common enemy.

Although the Nazi plan was to rid Europe of all Jews, irrespective
of their nation of origin, they were likely to meet pockets of resistance
if they implemented their programme too swiftly on the German
Jewish population as a whole. However, since we were in a different
category and were 'foreign' as well as Jewish, we were a soft target, so
their plan was to start by targeting 'foreign Jews' before tackling the
larger problem of the entire Jewish population in Germany.

On 28 October 1938, an order was issued for all Jewish men of
Polish origin to report to the police station. All men and boys had to
be 'registered' by the police. My father did not know what to do. If
you did not register, you were likely to be punished; and if you
registered, you were sure to be deported. We might not yet have known
the eventual destination of the deportees, but it seemed that whatever
choice my father made would put us in danger. We said goodbye to
my mother and left for the police station feeling very worried.

Most of my friends went to the local police station with their
fathers. Outside the station there were long, orderly queues. After all,
the Jews were law-abiding citizens so they waited to be told what to do

and where to go. In those queues, I saw the men of our community with their sons. I did not know then that I would never see them again.

My father was friendly with a local police officer. When he saw us among those gathered at the police station, he told my father to leave as unobtrusively and quickly as possible. He said he was certain that those once 'registered' would not be allowed to return home. The authorities were sending people straight to Poland without allowing them time to pack their possessions. At this point, my parents realised the urgency of our situation and began to make plans for our escape from Germany.

'Repatriation' in Poland

At the time, I wasn't fully aware of the situation in the rest of Germany. I only knew what was happening to us in Cologne. I did not know that all over Germany, Jews of Polish descent were being arrested and rounded up. The way in which they did this varied from area to area. In Cologne, as I remember, it was done without violence and initially, only all males were summoned to report to the local police station. In other areas, German police went to Jewish homes at night and issued the men with expulsion orders. The police then forced them to get dressed at once and escorted them to the Polish border. In some areas, complete families were expelled without prior warning.

Among those deported were elderly people who died on the journey, children and sick people. The Germans beat those who did not move quickly enough and then searched the refugees, confiscating most of the money they found, but allowing them to keep just ten marks.

The situation was so desperate for the refugees that some tried to escape back to Germany; others managed to find relatives in Poland with whom they could stay. But the vast majority were left in this 'no-man's-land' – expelled from Germany and refused entry to Poland by the Polish authorities. The Polish border town of Zbaszyn was the location where thousands of refugees found themselves without food and shelter and with no means of escape.

Among these refugees were the family of Herschel Grynszpan, and it was on hearing of the pitiful state in which his parents were living that he had decided to shoot the German diplomat, vom Rath.

The large-scale deportation of this group back to Poland was, for some, the first real indication not only that the Germans had no regard for our welfare, but also that they were no longer worried about

THE JEWISH TIMES — 4 —

Jewish Times English Section

Pitiful Position of Jewish Refugees

IN NO MAN'S LANDS ON POLISH-GERMAN FRONTIER.

According to reliable information received by Polish Jewish organisations, hundreds of Jews are at present wandering about in different "no man's lands" on the Polish-German frontier towns. There are many women and children among them. These Jews, former Polish citizens who have been deported from Germany, are usually driven to the frontier by Nazi guards in the dead of night under threats of being shot if they refused to obey Nazi orders.

Once on the Polish side of the frontier, they are usually rounded up by frontier guards with the help of blood hounds who attack them and drive them back across the German frontier, from where they are again driven back by force.

Relatives of the Zbonshyn refugees in Germany who were assured that in accordance with the Polish-German agreement they would be admitted to Poland, are also among these refugees and are refused admission by the Polish authorities.

The Polish side of the frontier is heavily guarded to prevent any of the Jews driven out of Germany from entering Poland.

Several cases of women among these refugees collapsing from exhaustion in the open fields with their little children lying by their sides are reported. Many small children are wandering about in these no man's lands in search of their parents. The refugees spend the nights under the open sky in fields and woods only to be roused by their pursuers and driven off on another aimless chase.

The problem of food is acute. Refugees are not provided with food on either the German or the Polish border points, because no facilities exist therefor. In the first days, while the refugees still had the 10 marks which the German Government allowed them to take, they were able to buy food from the wives of the Polish frontier guards. They have now, however, exhausted all their money and the refugees are literally starving. On the Polish side of the frontier they are usually given food by the Polish peasants, or by the Jews from the neighbouring townships. These refugees present a horrible and pitiful sight. Their faces are dirty, their clothes are bespattered and in tatters, their strength is being gradually sapped and many of them are seriously ill.

The only way to help these refugees, it is pointed out in informed circles here, is to establish temporary refugee camps in Poland, where they should be allowed to remain untill a place of refuge is found for them. Only such a step would bring temporary relief to hundreds of Jews who are at present hounded like animals over the Polish-German frontier.

Extract from a newspaper I kept, describing the fate of the Jews sent to Zbaszyn

international condemnation of their treatment of the Jews. By 31 October, the Polish authorities issued an order forbidding Jews to leave the town of Zbaszyn.

Despite the terrible conditions and high death rate among the refugees, the Jewish Aid Committee sent a group of Jews from Warsaw to Zbaszyn, and they set up a whole refugee town to help the thousands of stranded Jews. This included classes, a welfare office and a hospital.

In January 1939 an agreement was reached which allowed German Jews to return to Germany for a short time to "sort out their business affairs". The money from these would have been placed in accounts from which withdrawal would have been impossible. On 1 September 1939, Germany invaded Poland, condemning those Jews trapped in this border town to the same fate as the three million Jews in the rest of Poland.

LEAVING GERMANY

After Hitler came to power and throughout the 1930s, the number of Jews leaving Germany was rising. For our family, there was no obvious place for us to go to. I recall stories of people waiting for several years to obtain a visa and of difficult and traumatic journeys to foreign countries.

Thousands of Germans left for Palestine, but I remember hearing that the living conditions there were known to be very tough and I don't think my parents had any particular Zionistic aspirations at that time. Some of my older friends joined Zionist youth groups early in the 1930s. Later, they found ways of travelling to Palestine and started new lives there as pioneers. They started working in those tough conditions, draining the swamp lands; they then worked in agriculture and began *kibbutzim*, agricultural collectives.

Some people left for other parts of Europe and South America. I heard that people had gone to Cuba and wondered what possessed Polish Jews to go and settle there. I don't think that at that stage we really realised that they were escaping for their lives. The life they knew in Germany was comfortable and they were reluctant to give it up.

However, although we witnessed people leaving, there was also movement into Cologne from the surrounding areas. Jewish refugees from small towns and villages in the Rhineland, who had experienced persecution, moved to Cologne where they felt safer because the city had a larger Jewish population and a strong communal welfare system. This must have given those already living in Cologne a false sense of security. My parents probably also felt that they were likely to be better off in Cologne than elsewhere.

My brother Hermann, who was three years older than me, had already gone to live in England in 1937. He had gone with our first cousin, Max Winterfeld. Our cousin Adele was also allowed to travel to England since she had found employment as a 'domestic'.

Long before the events of 28 October 1938, my parents had made some contingency plans, but until we were actually called to the police station that day, my parents had been reluctant to use them. For years, there had been talk of us emigrating to America. We had relatives in America, the Weintraubs. This part of the family had emigrated from Poland to the USA and had agreed to be our guarantors.

Although we had visas to go to the USA, we did not have any immediate means of leaving Germany easily. We needed to obtain transit papers to travel to Britain. This was not a simple matter, but needed to be done very discreetly and quickly. My brother Hermann and my cousin Max Winterfeld travelled to Belgium with our passports and managed to get visas for travel to Britain for us all. They were very fortunate in finding an official who was happy to supply the papers immediately – in exchange for a small cash bribe. It is probably thanks to the actions of that unscrupulous civil servant that we survived!

I do not remember my father's reaction to having to leave Cologne, but I know that my parents felt reluctant to go. They had been very happy and comfortable in Germany and one of their main concerns was for my father's livelihood. In Germany, he had always been employed and had a decent salary. My mother cried a great deal about leaving our settled life. She was desperately sad at leaving her sister, Ronchi Winterfeld, to whom she was especially close.

A young man, well settled in London

TRAVELLING TO ENGLAND

The idea of sending me to England on my own must have been quite difficult for my parents. I was only 16 years old. It was a significant journey by rail and sea and I had not travelled that far without them before. My parents' plan was that I would travel first, and that they would organise a few things in Cologne and then join me in England. In particular, they wanted to pack up all the furniture and household goods so that they could have them shipped over to England. In the event, they did pack everything up and arranged a shipment, but mysteriously their belongings never arrived!

Late in 1938, I travelled via Holland to Harwich and then to Dover. There were many young Jewish people travelling on the same route. As I remember it, there were many Austrian teenagers on the boat. There were Jewish teenagers from all over Europe whose parents had somehow managed to send them to safety.

Some of the youngsters were travelling en route to New York and some hoped to settle in London. On the journey, I struck up a friendship with a Viennese girl who was a few years older than me.

Regina Rosenzweig had come from Austria and was on her way to New York. I think she thought we had a future together. She certainly was my girlfriend in 1938-9. I still have her photograph and some of the letters that she wrote to me. But she went to live in New York and I stayed in London and whatever plans we might have had never came to anything!

England was not envisaged as our family's long-term destination. It was to be a stage in our journey on the way to New York, where we were to join our relatives, the Weintraubs. In the event, I reached England before my parents and quickly became accustomed to my new life. After my parents arrived in England, the subject of moving to the USA did not come up again. I think they were keen to put down roots. We had all experienced enough upheaval and were keen to settle in London.

LIFE IN LONDON, 1938

In November 1938, I was 16 years old and found myself living in Stamford Hill, North London. My brother Hermann was already living there, in the home of a Jewish widow and her daughter. Mrs Kay was a cook in a restaurant – and she was a great cook. I came to join him there and had to share a bedroom with Miss Kay, who worked as a secretary for the Weintraub family, some of whom were living in London. I do not think that we paid the Kays for our board and lodging. I think that they were kind and hospitable to us because they recognised the difficulty of our situation.

At first I was very homesick; I missed all the home comforts and the friends I had left behind. I had left a whole world to which we would never return. It was much later that I came to realise that we were incredibly fortunate to have left Germany when we did. Had we left it any later, our fate would undoubtedly have been like that of the vast majority of our friends and family who were sent to be 'repatriated' in Poland.

My brother had a job and was busy during the day. My parents were waiting to organise their furniture in Germany, so I was alone in a foreign country with no work and nothing to occupy me during the day. I had always been interested in cabinet-making and had wanted to train as a carpenter in Cologne. I had learnt some basic carpentry at the craft school set up by the Cologne Jewish community. Initially, my English was very rudimentary; we had learnt some English at school, but I am sure I was far from fluent.

Despite this, I found my first job in a furniture factory in London's East End. It was more like an apprenticeship than a real job. I was there for a few months and during that time Regina, the Viennese girl I had met on the way to London, used to come and meet me for lunch. This was a great comfort to me as I was very lonely in an unfamiliar environment, without my parents and my friends from home.

The factory where I worked when I arrived in England

48

Early in 1939, my parents arrived in London and we were able to rent a first-floor flat in a house in Ilford. This was certainly an improvement in living conditions for me. I got a job as a delivery boy with Mr Samuel, the kosher butcher. I was given a bicycle which had a large basket on the front. Every day, this was piled high with fresh chickens and meat, which I would deliver around Ilford. I enjoyed this job; Mr Samuel was very good to me and we became friends. I worked five and a half days a week and received a wage of £3 per week. I was a very trusted employee and was given the key to the shop and often had to open up in the morning and lock up at night. The job also had its perks – every week I was given two fresh chickens on Friday, so I was able to provide the *Shabbat* meal for my parents!

After that, I worked at a clothing factory in the city. This involved checking army uniforms with a foreman standing over us who inspected our work. I distinctly remember measuring and checking khaki trousers as they came off the production line and stamping them with the stamp from the War Office. I was always a very quick and thorough worker. We were employed to do piecework and were paid for the amount of work we did. Since I was fast, I earned a decent salary. I worked from eight till five and the journey each way was about half an hour on the trolley bus.

Letters from Friends

In the summer of 1939, I was getting used to life in London, but I was homesick and missing my friends in Cologne. In a letter sent by my friend Jetta Hofrichter, she tries to comfort me and refers to a poem about Cologne by Willi Ostermann, a German poet we had studied in school.

I was born in Cologne on the Rhine
And this is very important for me
I haven't lost my mother tongue
And I am proud of that.

So when I think of my homeland
And… about the cathedral
Then I'd like to turn round and go back home
I want to go to Cologne on foot.

And if the good Lord calls me
Then I'll say to St Peter

Then I can really tell you
I am homesick for Cologne.

This poem reflected our feelings for our home town and for Germany. We felt deeply rooted in Germany and had a sense of belonging and patriotism. At the time, we simply could not imagine that the country in which we had built our lives would reject us so forcefully. Cologne was the place on which we had pinned all our youthful hopes and dreams. It was unthinkable that from the very culture in which we lived, a system would emerge that would eventually destroy our culture and our people.

It is over 60 years since I last looked at the letters my friends sent to me when I was living in London. The content of dozens of letters, all sent between December 1938 and February 1940, is evidence of their terrible story. I cannot forget my overwhelming feeling of helplessness at the time. However much I tried, and however much I wanted to, I was unable to save my friends. Even now, reading these letters fills me with distress.

But these letters tell a story that has to be told. Today, they are all that I have to remind me of the friends from my youth in Cologne. Although many of the letters are chatty and tell me of everyday matters, beneath the optimistic veneer, the details convey utter desperation. They are sent to me in London from different locations in Germany, Belgium and Poland, from places where my friends found themselves in their lonely attempts to survive. All have a central theme, the need to find an escape route from the Nazis. Wherever they are, all are confronted with a different bureaucratic obstacle course from which there is no way out. New regulations and restrictions are constantly imposed on them, making an escape impossible. As the letters become more frequent, they also become more desperate as borders are closed and exits blocked.

In the year prior to the outbreak of war, thousands of Jews were trying to leave Germany and Poland. In many cases, it was impossible for whole families to leave together. Because of this many parents were forced to make the agonising decision to separate from their children and try to send them to safety in the hope that one day they might be reunited.

Parents in this situation had limited time and few options. There were two possible ways in which young people could be permitted to travel to England. There was the *Kindertransport* organisation which arranged the transport and placement of Jewish refugee children from places in Nazi-occupied Europe in Britain. But this was only for children under the age of 17. And only a small number were able to escape this way.

The other possibility for many of my contemporaries was to obtain a permit to travel to Britain in order to work as a domestic. Before they were able to secure a permit, they needed to find a position. For this reason, I received many requests from friends who were threatened with deportation to Poland to help find them posts, so that they could travel to Britain. The work for the lucky few who did manage to find it was often back-breaking menial work at a fixed rate of pay of 15 shillings a week. Many highly skilled German refugees came to England and worked as domestics. Despite the loss of status and irrespective of the nature of the work, the Jewish refugees were in no doubt that for them this was the best option.

In those months before the outbreak of war, I used to travel on a daily basis from my home in Ilford, Essex, to Woburn House in central London in a desperate attempt to help my friends.

Woburn House was the headquarters of the Jewish community, the building which housed the office of the Chief Rabbi and many important communal organisations. During the 1930s, Woburn House became the centre for the Jewish Refugee Committee, the place where the Jewish community attempted to find ways of helping the thousands of refugees from Nazi-occupied Europe. They had some success at organising the safe passage of young refugees to Palestine. They helped place *Kindertransport* children and find work and homes for older children. But sadly, by the beginning of 1939, the situation for Jews in Germany and Poland was desperate. There were hundreds of volunteers trying to deal with the bureaucracy. As my letters show, I would always write back to those who had written to me. I tried to find work for my friends; I queued for hours and spent many days talking to people at Woburn House who wanted to help, but none of my efforts yielded results. I didn't know it then, but now I realise that there was absolutely nothing I could do to save my friends.

✡ ✡ ✡

HELMA'S STORY

The story of Helma Ascher, a friend from Aachen, presents a microcosm of the story of European Jewry in the 1930s. Until 1938, Helma worked for Dr Blum, a Jewish doctor, at his home. However, from 1933 Jewish doctors were not permitted to practise and it is not clear how Dr Blum made a living in those years. On 17 December 1938, he wrote a job reference for Helma, including the fact that *"unfortunately I must sell my house so I have to release her from service."*

After this, Helma was employed in the kitchen of a Jewish hotel and indeed in March 1939, she received a glowing reference from her employer, Helen Schloss of the Schloss Hotel, confirming her qualities of being "hard-working and honest". However, by this stage there was no need for a Jewish hotel in Germany and consequently Mrs Schloss was forced to let Helma go, due to *"lack of work"*.

Helma wrote to me on 18 March 1939, thanking me for writing to her. *"You do seem to be the first one who keeps his word and will do something for me…"* She enclosed photographs of herself, a CV, her birth certificate and character references. All these documents had been painstakingly collected. She also asked me to send them back to her if I was unable to help her because *"to replace these costs a lot of money"*. She asked me to try to help find work for her in England and went on to tell me about her situation. She also told me the following:

> *My parents are likely to emigrate to Cuba in about two months. It would be good if I could be away by then, because otherwise I will be alone here… I have not got any more relatives…*

This was the last letter I received from Helma. Despite her determination and all her efforts, she was unable to find a safe escape route. I heard nothing further from her, so I do not know what happened to her between 1939 and 1942.

She perished in Auschwitz on 5 November 1942. She was just 22.

PEREZ' STORY

Recently, I found a cutting that I had kept from a Jewish newspaper of 1939. The report describes the plight of the Jews abandoned and imprisoned in Zbaszyn, Poland:

> *These refugees present a pitiful sight. Their faces are dirty, their clothes are in tatters… their strength is being sapped and many of them are seriously ill.*

This was the fate that my friend Perez was keen to avoid; he knew that Jews were being sent to *"no-man's-land"*. Somehow, he also knew that this was likely to be a death sentence.

Most of my friends were Jews of Polish descent who were living in Germany. In 1939, as the Nazis began heaping ever-more restrictive laws on the Jews, they decided to target those who had come from Poland after the First World War. Many of my friends and their families were in that category. If they held Polish passports that had expired, they had the added complication of not being admitted into Poland. This must have been the situation of my friend Perez Ruwalski, who writes of his fear of being stranded in *"no-man's-land"*.

Perez had been a classmate from our early years in Cologne and was with me later in the craft school run by the Jewish community. He wrote to me every few days from May until July 1939. His parents also wrote letters to me during that period. Perez' letter to my family on 19 May 1939 opens with the words:

I beg you, please help me in our dangerous situation, because it is urgent… We can only stay here until 15 July.

In this letter, he writes that he has been desperately trying to get relatives in London to help him in his plight. He has also been telegraphing Woburn House in London so that he can get the relevant documents to enable him to leave Germany.

We have had the same promises from Woburn House, so please be kind enough to act now as there is still time to do so…

Perez knows that his family are in great danger of being sent back to Poland. Unlike some others, he seems to be fully aware that this is a death sentence for his family.

In his letter of 2 July 1939, he begs me to find his relative who lives in London and go with him to Woburn House. He is desperate and pleads:

All I want you to do is go with your father to my uncle… He will receive you pleasantly as he is a good person. He has dealt with the matter of our permit. But it has already taken four months and we haven't a glimmer of hope of coming to London… Do it as a Mensch, as a Jew, do your duty for others…

He also reminds me that my father made a promise to his father.

There are many letters asking us to help through intervention at Woburn House on his behalf. I am not sure that we were in a position to help him although I am sure we tried. In one letter his mother writes:

If, G-d forbid, you can't help us then at least do something for my son.

Sadly, I was not able to help Perez or fulfil Mrs Ruwalksi's request. Like most of my school friends, Perez perished in Auschwitz in 1942.

FRIEDEL'S STORY

Another friend from Cologne, Friedel Sternlicht, was still in Cologne in July 1939. Her family had a visa to travel to America, but the German authorities would not let them travel. Waiting in utter desperation in Cologne, she fears the threat of being forcibly sent back to Poland and writes:

Yes, Leo, you know how one gets separated from people and who knows if one will ever meet again? These are the blows of fate... If it is possible for you to look after me then I would never forget you…

Sadly, Friedel never managed to use her visa to travel to America. She was forcibly repatriated to Poland. Friedel perished in the Lodz ghetto.

THE HOFRICHTERS' STORY

My closest friend in Cologne was Fredi Hofrichter. He was just six days younger than me and we were inseparable. His family lived in the same apartment block as ours and the families were close. We were part of a group of boys who went everywhere together. I was also friendly with his older brother, Rudi, and his younger sister, Jetta. Jetta was a lovely girl with red hair who always had a good word for everyone. Fredi and Rudi managed to get to Belgium in 1939. The rest of the family were left in Cologne. In 1939, Mrs Hofrichter was unwell and needed hospital treatment in Cologne. This was terrible for the family as it prevented them from joining the two older children in Belgium.

Among the letters I have are many from Jetta. On 18 June 1939, she writes that she is trying to get all the relevant documentation together to get work as a domestic in England.

However, like many Jews of Polish origin, they are forced to go to Poland. Because of Mrs Hofrichter's medical treatment, the family are 'permitted' a longer stay in Cologne until 28 June 1939. But after this, they are forced to travel to Poland. Jetta writes with sadness that they have to take her younger brother with them to Poland because by this time *"the Kindertransports have ceased"*.

Despite the situation, all of Jetta's letters reflect an optimistic personality and incredible concern for the well-being of everyone. In spite of the family's desperate wish to be together, she bravely accepts that they must go Poland.

We would have preferred to go to Rudi and Fredi but as you know, it does not depend on us. If things go well for us, then they will go well for us in Poland…

It seems that the Hofrichters actually stayed in Cologne until 2 July 1939, when Jetta writes to me saying that she has gathered together all the important papers to organise her journey to England. She is also very gracious in thanking me for taking the trouble to correspond with her brothers, who are in a refugee camp in Belgium.

I am glad you have written to the boys… You know what it is like in foreign parts without parents… They are having a bad time and we cannot help them…

In this letter she reflects that:

Nowadays everyone is torn from one another and one does not know when one will ever meet again. These are cruel blows of fate. One has to take everything as it comes… But we all hope that we will meet again in happiness… One must not allow courage to fade.

Jetta's last letter to me from Cologne carefully lists all the documentation she has accumulated. This includes her school report, birth certificate and character reference. On each occasion, she cannot write a lot because of the expense of sending a heavier letter. She refers to the fact that I am trying to find a post for her in London.

I am very happy that you are going to settle everything, so I can go to Poland calmly…

However, before she leaves Germany, she says:

I will often think back to Cologne in every aspect… I really do not want to go to Poland, but am left with no choice. Tomorrow I am off and I will only describe the good things to you.

She also tells me that she has written to her beloved older brothers in Belgium:

The letter I wrote was a farewell letter for now. Who knows when we will be together with them?

By 19 July 1939, Jetta is in Lvov (Lemberg), Poland. She describes how her family spent some time in the border town of Zbaszyn:

…where we had some really lovely days… I met a lot of people from Cologne…

and the culture and social difference between Cologne and Lvov:

Here it is difficult to find work – there are more poor people than rich ones. At the moment we are staying with relatives… but in the long term we cannot stay here because they do not have much.

Jetta is shocked by the poverty that she witnesses:

You really cannot imagine how the Jewish quarter looks. We simply cannot get used to living here. We think back longingly to our time in Cologne – a time that will never come back.

Clearly, although the Hofrichter family were originally from Poland, they had not lived in Poland and did not even speak Polish. Like thousands who were forced out of Germany, they found their forced 'repatriation' incredibly difficult.

It is very difficult to get work here. My father has had a few casual jobs, but he cannot speak Polish, so he can't make himself understood anywhere. Those who receive help from the refugee committee are only given enough to cover the most basic necessities. Here the people do not have the slightest sympathy for the refugees. Please believe me when I say I am terribly unhappy about my stay here. I have no one with whom to speak in German. I have faith that the future will be better. I will not allow myself to lose faith.

Despite all this, Jetta tries to keep occupied during the day and is optimistic about her hope of finding work in England:

During the day I go sightseeing and look at the big buildings and the streets of Lemberg. The University of Lemberg is a wonderful building… I am longing for the day when I can start my journey, because to stay here is impossible for me.

The Hofrichters had wanted to join their sons in Belgium, but as these letters show, hope for Jews all over Europe was fading fast. Jetta writes:

It is good we did not go to Belgium. Today we received a letter with the following information:

The refugees who arrived after 30 April 1939 must all leave Belgium within four weeks. Rudi and Fredi had permission to remain there but had to agree to go to another camp. They had just managed to get a bit of work when they received this blow...

The content of Jetta's letters fluctuates between hope and despair:

Here there is talk that there is going to be a war. Is that the case? My mother was not allowed to stay in Germany to complete her convalescence. Have you found any jobs for me yet? Mammi [her younger brother] is not at school and is missing his friends.

This was the last letter I received from Jetta and her parents on 8 August 1939. I certainly wrote to them after I received this letter, and their sons Rudi and Fredi wrote to them from Belgium, but sadly none of us heard anything more from them.

However, despite not knowing the precise fate of my friends, the Hofrichters, I do know that the entire Jewish population of Lvov was obliterated over the next three years. The terrible fate of the Jews of Lvov at that time is well documented.

On 17 September 1939, just a month after Jetta sent her last letter to me, the Soviet Army moved into Lvov. At this time, Lvov had a Jewish population of 110,000, but as the Soviet forces moved into the town, thousands more Jews from German-occupied areas of western Poland also escaped to this area.

On 3 September 1940, a German bomb made a direct hit on Krotka Street, the precise street in which the Hofrichters lived. In this attack, dozens of Jews in this heavily populated street were killed.

From 30 June 1941, German military forces occupied Lvov. The Ukrainians and the Germans killed 4,000 Jews in that month. This was followed by a series of pogroms of indescribable brutality, the shooting of 5,000 sick and elderly Jews and the creation of a sealed ghetto in Lvov. Survivors after these pogroms were transported to Belzec extermination camp. The remaining Jews from Belzec were sent to Janowska labour camp. On 5 January 1943, 10,000 Jews were shot in a ravine outside the city. On 1 June 1943, the Germans declared the operation to clear Lvov of its Jewish population to be complete.

FREDI AND RUDI IN BELGIUM

On 27 July 1939, my friend Fredi Hofrichter wrote to me from Belgium. At that stage, he knows that his parents, sister and brother are living with his uncle in Lvov. He is still trying to enjoy his time in Belgium and writes about the boxing championships that he is going to watch. But he is not allowed to participate *"because I am a foreigner"*.

On 29 February 1940, Rudi Hofrichter writes to me expressing his distress about having no news from his family in Lvov:

Above all I am so happy at how much effort you make to find out about my parents. The fact that the registered letter you sent was not successful reduced even the faintest hope that I might receive news from my dear parents. Where could fate have led them?

Far too soon Fredi and I have had to learn that the whole world has abandoned us. This is a tragic and unhappy time. We could not have been hit harder. Just think, dear Leo, that Fredi is a young boy who needs parental love and nurturing. Although we were much trouble for our parents, our love and efforts were only for them. But not that long ago, we did not know what it meant to be alone in the world and left to our own resources. Now we are so sorry. We have cried our eyes out and were near to despair. The only hope we could get was a sign of life from them. We must stay close together so that we are not entirely wiped out. We ask ourselves, what is our future and how will it end?

Rudi goes on to describe his life in the refugee camp:

Here in the camp, there is no possibility of leaving or travelling anywhere. The standard of the food has gone down. There is no money to buy raw materials. We have learnt to be cobblers, but there is no leather so we have no work. We have become good at speaking French, perhaps one day this will be useful for us. Our relatives have left us totally without support. At least we are happy that you are alright in London...

The last letter I received from the Hofrichter brothers was written on 29 April 1940. Ironically, this letter is full of hope:

We have been moved to another camp near Brussels and we have the most comfortable rooms. When the summer comes, it will be lovely here because the grounds offer great opportunities. The schooling has come to an abrupt end…

At the end of the letter, Fredi asks me to help him get some clothes, because all his are threadbare after years as a refugee.

I don't remember exactly when I received this last communication from my closest friend. But less than two weeks after he wrote his last letter to me, the Germans invaded Belgium. After that, the Hofrichters were likely to have been subjected to the full impact of Nazi rule. There were many refugees living in Belgium who had fled from Germany, Poland and Austria. Although they had escaped from the Nazis in their home towns, the Nazis were determined to hunt them down wherever they were. Between August 1942 and July 1944, 25,000 Jews who had been living in Belgium were deported to their deaths.

Sadly, Rudi and Fredi were among this group. According to records, Fredi perished in Auschwitz and it is likely that Rudi, his protective older brother, was with him till the end of his short life.

Aged 23 in uniform

Training with the RAOC. I am in the back row, second from the right.

LIFE IN THE RAOC

Had my parents known of my burning ambition to become a British fighter pilot, with one clear wish – to bomb Cologne Cathedral – they would probably have locked me in my bedroom of 59 Mansfield Road, Ilford!

Although I enjoyed living and working in London and always tried to be the dutiful son, in reality, I was burning with anger against the Nazis and what they had done to our home town. I had also become British and felt that I wanted to play my part in the war effort. In 1944, I heard about British soldiers flying to Germany and not being able to locate their precise targets. Some of these young pilots had attempted to return with their ammunition, but never made the return journey and were blown up by their own ammunition. These events, combined with my memories of the Nazis on the streets of my home town of Cologne, made me determined to have an active role in the army.

I went to the air force headquarters in Romford to enrol. But unfortunately, I was required to have a full medical. To my regret, my flat feet made me unsuitable to be a pilot. I was labelled a B2. I felt this was a severe blow. In retrospect, it might have been very fortunate for me. My parents would have been delighted that I was not to become the pilot of a fighter plane, but I was a young man full of ambition and was bitterly disappointed.

So I accepted my fate, became enrolled in the Royal Army Ordinance Corps (RAOC) and worked as an interpreter. My tasks involved translating German documents into English and interpreting for the army. It was a very safe desk job and a far cry from the exciting role that I had hoped for.

I enjoyed my time in the RAOC, although it was not very demanding. We were generally good friends with the other soldiers from the Royal West Kent Regiment, with whom we shared a base in Maidstone, Kent. But I was one of just three Jewish boys. When my comrades queued up for bacon and eggs for breakfast, I opted just to have the eggs! I did not experience any antisemitism or even any antipathy to me because I was German. At that stage, my accent must have been very pronounced. But in general, people were good-natured and we were working together on a common cause.

I remember just one case when a sergeant was a bit aggressive and swore at me in an unprovoked attack. I told him firmly that I had chosen to volunteer, whereas he had been conscripted. I think I had a tremendous amount of self-belief and this must have come across. Later, this sergeant behaved in a very civilised manner towards me and I never encountered other problems.

The RAOC had other compensations. I was not far from home and was not doing a difficult or dangerous job. There were lots of ATS (Auxiliary Territorial Service) girls with whom I became very friendly. I had leave and was allowed to go home for many weekends and for a young man, it was a happy time.

When the war ended, there were huge celebrations on the streets in the centre of London. There were street parties and all over England, the girls were going crazy because their boys were coming home.

But the reality was not so glorious. The boys who had survived did not come home immediately. And many never came back. In the Jewish community there were no great celebrations.

Curiously, I don't remember hearing about what had happened to our family in Poland ever. Nor do I remember my parents talking about the situation of the thousands of displaced persons. I know now that the newspapers were full of stories about what the Russians found when they liberated Auschwitz; and what the British saw when they arrived at Bergen-Belsen, and the Americans at Buchenwald. Yet somehow this whole horrific history was not part of the discussions at our home in Ilford.

My parents must have known about it, but discussions centred on domestic and family matters and nothing that unimaginable was ever even touched upon.

I am not sure when we last heard from our cousins, the Winterfelds. I know that the family were sent back to Poland. My uncle Chaim went back to Stanislawow with some of his children in 1939. He went into the leather business there and probably worked in that way for two years. Beyond that information, although I have tried to find out more specific details of what happened to the family, sadly, my attempts have not been successful.

The story of the Jews of Stanislawow is similar to that of the fate of Jews in hundreds of towns and villages in Eastern Europe.

In 1941 there were about 40,000 Jews in Stanislawow. On 26 July 1941, the Nazis arrived and gathered the Jews in the market square. They then escorted them to the Jewish cemetery, where graves had been dug for them. Between 8,000 and 12,000 Jews were shot on that day. A further series of *Aktions* took place. On 22 August 1942, the

Nazis held a reprisal *Aktion* for the murder of a Ukrainian, which they blamed on a Jew. More than 1,000 Jews were shot.

By February 1943, there were 11,000 Jews remaining in the ghetto. Oskar Brandt, who had succeeded Hans Kruger as the *SS Hauptsturmführer*, ordered the police to surround the ghetto, initiating its final liquidation. Four days after the beginning of this *Aktion*, the Germans put up posters declaring that Stanislawow was rid of its Jews.

When Soviet forces arrived on 27 July 1944, there were about 100 Jews who had survived the war in hiding. Historians estimate that only about 1,500 of the original 40,000 Jews living in the area survived the war. It is difficult to know any precise numbers with certainty because of the swift and brutal nature of the elimination of Jews in this region. In areas like Stanislawow, the Jews were murdered quickly and brutally, with the cooperation of the local forces. Unlike in the concentration camps where the Germans kept meticulous records, no records were kept and so no traces have been found.

✡ ✡ ✡

Outside my RAOC living quarters, 1946

FAMILY, FRIENDS AND THE REST...

With the benefit of hindsight, I was incredibly lucky to be a young man in my early twenties at the end of the war. Like many of my generation, there was no inclination to look back and dwell on the past and what had been lost. At the time, I was full of drive and enthusiasm and was keen to make my way in the world. I was particularly fortunate to have the opportunity to join the costume jewellery business that employed my cousin Max Winterfeld and my brother Hermann.

As well as my ambitions to progress commercially, my social life and involvement with the local Jewish community were always of great importance. I always had a very strong sense of my Jewish identity. Keeping in tune with Jewish traditions was a central part in my life.

Ever since arriving in Britain, I felt it was important that young Jewish people should have the opportunity to socialise with each other. In Cologne, the society in which we lived had consisted entirely of Jewish friends and neighbours.

The life of a working man in London was in sharp contrast to my previously sheltered existence. In London, I was in a totally new environment; I was working during the day. I felt that unless I created the opportunity for myself, I would not mix with Jewish people of my own age. At the time, there was a network of clubs, called Young Israel. Its headquarters were in Woburn House, central London, but it had branches in different districts of London.

During the war, I set up and became chairman of the Ilford branch of Young Israel. We had a committee to organise events, a secretary, Margaret Samuels, and a treasurer, Cecil Richards. We had 200 members and our offices were on the first floor of Ilford Federation synagogue. We organised cultural events and went on excursions such as river cruises.

Club river cruise on the Thames, 1947; Freda and Leon already a couple

AROUND THE SOCIETIES—continued

HOUNSLOW

As every reader will doubtlessly have heard how well Hounslow Y.I. is progressing in every branch of its activities, it will be quite unnecessary for me to elaborate on that theme in this report.

I would, however, like to acquaint you with some of our more recent successes and with our plans for the future.

A discussion with the title "Current Affairs," ably led by MR. S. GREENE, one of our Vice-Presidents, proved most interesting and gave us all a chance to express our views on many subjects, including politics and economics.

Drama has been progressing favourably and regular rehearsals are taking place. The first ramble of the season was noted a complete success—in fact the organisation showed a hint of the "Montgomery-Eisenhower" touch, so well was it carried out. We all eagerly await the next outdoor function.

Now for our future programme. Firstly, a "pedal-pushing" day, led by Betty, the Society's Sports Chairman. May the sun shine upon us and no punctures mar our joy.

Musical appreciation ranks high on our list of forthcoming events and will no doubt be enjoyed by all.

The highlight of the May programe is a discussion led by REV. J. FERBER, with "The Orthodox versus The Liberal Synagogue" as its subject. I am sure we shall all learn much from the evening's happenings.

By the time this report appears in print, the first issue of the Society's journal "Hounslow Y.I. Topics" will have been published. We hope to make this a regular monthly feature and look forward to receiving YOUR contribution to its pages.

There I must leave you—but more from Hounslow in the next issue.

ARNOLD E. BENSUSAN,
Publicity Officer.

ILFORD

Before I commence my report may I say how very pleased I am to be writing to you again as Chairman of I.Y.I., after a lapse of some years due to my service in H.M. Forces.

I was more than gratified to see the Y.I. spirit was still in evidence in the Club, as I left it.

My Committee is very able and hardworking and I am indeed happy to have their co-operation, so that we may work as a team to further the interest of Jewish youth in the district.

Our Motto shall be "WE WILL SERVE," and we shall endeavour to obtain the high standard we have set ourselves.

I have noticed of late a certain lack of support at all our functions especially our Wednesday nights, while hoping that this may be due to the fine weather; may I assure you that we have worked hard to produce a most varied and interesting programme for the summer months one which needs your full co-operation to ensure its success.

Our April programme boasted a number of literary events, the most outstanding of which proved to be the talk on Friendly Societies by Mr. H. S. Schildkraut.

Another highlight was "Focus Point," which will be held once monthly in future, when current topics will be discussed.

I am happy to announce the co-option on to the committee of JEFF GOLDING in whose capable hands I am entrusting the Sports Section. He has arranged a splendid programme for the next few months and I beg you—support him to the full.

The I.Y.I. has had many changes of fortune in the past few years and I want you to remember that it is up to each and everyone of you to make the Club a success.

With your support we can go far —WITHOUT YOU—we fail.

I know you will not let me down.

LEON SCHALLER,
Chairman.

16

One evening in 1946, when we had our club meeting I noticed this strikingly pretty girl waiting outside the door. I asked her what she was doing and she told me she was waiting for her boyfriend.

I told her not to wait for him and offered to take her inside. I introduced myself as the chairman of the organisation. Her name was Freda Zaltsman and she also lived locally in Ilford. I gave her special treatment and a seat in the front row of the hall. I did not know it at the time, but that evening Freda went home and told her parents that she had met the young man she would eventually marry!

That night, the local rabbi was giving a lecture to our group. Curiously, I do not remember the lecture or its subject, but I do recall that when the talk was over, the rabbi spoke to the pretty lady whom I had seated in the front row. It turned out that he knew her family and so I decided to ask him some subtle questions about her.

Although I was unaware of it at the time, some days later, the rabbi went to see Freda's father, Mr Zaltsman, who was a tailor, at his shop. The rabbi helpfully suggested to him that I would be an appropriate *shidduch* (match) for Freda.

Since I had the blessing of the rabbi and consequently of Freda's father, we started seeing each other regularly and were soon courting quite seriously. Freda was a hairdresser and worked with her sister in Ilford. On Sundays, I used to borrow her father's Morris Minor and drive to town to take her out to the pictures. We both loved music and were keen dancers, so I would also take her for dinner dances at the Trocadero ballroom.

Very early on in our relationship, I knew that Freda was the girl for me. We had very similar values; she was very warm and family-minded and had a very close relationship with her parents. Like our family, the Zaltsmans were a Jewish family of Polish descent. Although her family had settled in England before ours, we had a great deal in common. Freda was kind and hard-working and devoted to the people close to her. I knew that she would be a great mother and would be happy to run a traditional Jewish home. Above all, she had an amazing love of life and we always laughed together.

In my mind, I had plans to get married to Freda, but only when I felt able to buy somewhere to live and support her. I had very definite ideas about what I wanted for the future. I wanted a home and a family and I

Freda aged 23, 1946

wanted Freda's place to be at the centre of our home. I hoped that once I could provide for her, she would be happy to give up hairdressing.

After a few months, we were driving together into town and she told me that her parents had asked her whether we were going to get engaged. I think they thought I was taking too long to propose to their daughter! I was never someone who liked being told what to do. So without saying anything, I turned the car round and headed back to her parents' house. Freda was a bit surprised – she had been hoping to see a movie!

I was not going to be pressurised, nor did I want Freda to be upset. So I drove back to her parents' house and I remember exactly what I said to them:

> *I understand you are nagging your daughter about our plans for the future. Let me make it quite clear. As soon as I feel able to make a decent living to support your daughter, I will propose to her.*

After this clarification, I enjoyed a wonderful relationship with Mr and Mrs Zaltsman. In reality, they did not have to wait too long as Freda and I got engaged in 1947.

Freda and I were married on 30 June 1948 in Hendon Synagogue and held the dinner at Hendon Hall Hotel. Rabbi Dr Lehrmann from Stamford Hill officiated and Reverend Hass was the cantor who sang for us under the *chuppa*.

I remember it was a blazing hot, stunning, summer's day and Freda looked more beautiful than I ever remembered her. I was overjoyed that we were able to start our lives together.

As we set off for a honeymoon in Capri, I did not know that this was the beginning of a marriage that was to last nearly 60 years and bring us the joy of three children, Malcolm, Clive and Linda.

Freda and I on our wedding day, 30 June 1948

Our showroom in Hainault, 1985

At Frankfurt Trade Fair, 1995

Leon Schaller and Sons

Looking back on my life, it seems incredible that in 1946 I managed to join a business that was to thrive and develop. Of course, I did not know then that my business would be able to help support three generations of my family and would preoccupy me for the next 60 years.

In the year after the war ended, the country was just beginning to normalise, but the effects of the war were felt in every area of national life. There was great austerity and rationing on many goods. But as well as the hardship people felt and the losses they had endured, the post-war years were also a time of great optimism. A new Britain was being built after the war and somehow our business fitted in with this new mood of the time.

Nowadays, people often ask me how I became such a successful businessman. The truth is that I don't really know why some things just worked for us from the beginning. I think that in many ways we were fortunate from the start. Perhaps in the post-war years, we provided something cheap and cheerful that brightened up people's lives without costing much.

Our business – costume jewellery – began as a fledgling company that then started to develop rapidly. In the late 1940s, plastic was just starting to be a widely available product. It was cheap and easy to mass-produce. Costume jewellery was becoming popular and since there was still rationing on clothing until 1949, perhaps it provided women with a way of updating old clothes.

At the beginning there were just three of us – my cousin Max Winterfeld, myself and my brother Hermann. We began by renting a warehouse in Waltham Abbey. For me, it was a totally new venture. The idea had originated because my cousin and my brother had both worked for our relatives, the Weintraubs, but they had gone to America after the war.

Both Hermann and Max used their experience to develop our company, which we called Shallwin Novelties, a name incorporating our surnames – Schaller and Winterfeld. The warehouse that we rented was soon turned into a factory. Initially, we manufactured a narrow range of products and employed a small number of staff to work on the factory floor, assembling necklaces, bracelets and earrings. Sometimes we found it was more cost-effective to buy wholesale beads from suppliers and assemble the jewellery at our factory. We all had different roles; Max oversaw the production line; Hermann and I were the salesmen.

We were making a small profit and so decided to invest in a plastic-moulding machine to manufacture beads. We started to make fake pearls that were moulded on a string. We soon made these in varying lengths, with different-sized pearls. We made earrings of many designs and a variety of designs of brooches that became very popular.

After a few years, Max left to start his own shop, selling handbags and leather goods. Later, my brother Hermann decided to go his own way and so I became independent.

However, the transition to become independent and acquire new premises was not an easy one. In order to buy the new factory, I had to borrow the money from the bank and as I had no capital, we had to guarantee the loan against the value of our house. Freda and I spent many sleepless nights wondering whether the risk would pay off. In business, you have to take risks and in order to expand, we needed to borrow, but the thought of losing our home haunted me for many years. I could only do this with Freda's encouragement, and although she also experienced her share of sleepless nights, she encouraged me at every turn. We were both determined that the business would succeed.

Freda was involved in all the major decisions I made concerning the business. When I became independent, I put Freda down as the Secretary and all my children's names were down as Directors. This was long before Malcolm, Clive and Linda were able to direct anything! But my vision was always that this would be a family-run business.

I loved running my own business and called it Leon Schaller and Sons Limited. I thrived on the buzz of business. I knew most of the managers of the shops who were my customers. I enjoyed meeting with directors and travelling. Our company grew rapidly and we obtained new premises in Hainault. Part of our company, Aloha Pearls, supplied Woolworths and before long, many girls in the country could be seen wearing our jewellery.

As in all businesses, the trick is to identify a trend and start to offer the public something just as it is becoming fashionable. Maybe I had a good eye, or perhaps it was my instincts, but I would travel around England and see what the big chain stores were selling. I would buy samples and then adapt and imitate designs. We were probably cheaper than our competitors.

I never tired of the thrill of selling. I had a simple strategy: if we had a new line, I tried it on 40 specimen Woolworths' shops first. This was a very good way of testing the market. If the line was a success, it would be sold to 2,000 shops. In this way, we never produced goods that did not sell and ensured that we always made a significant profit.

From the 1960s onwards, the whole business was geared around Woolworths, which at the time was a successful national chain with a very diverse range of products. For our company, being Woolworths' supplier offered us tremendous scope to develop and diversify.

Over the years, our business grew and expanded. In the early 1970s, we moved from selling jewellery to sourcing and distributing umbrellas and sunglasses. I had a loyal staff of three – Karen, my secretary, and Jane and Pam, who worked on sourcing and collating samples. There were another 30 staff dealing with invoices and working in the warehouse. All our staff worked hard; enormous quantities of goods were managed by a relatively small staff.

Meanwhile, I was constantly seeing the buyers at the Head Office of Woolworths in Marylebone Road. I would pick up ideas from the buyers as to what the customers might want next. Then I would feed the ideas back to my staff who would source them. I was always after the excitement of finding something new and providing it at the most competitive price on the High Street.

In those days, I would take the buyers out regularly to discuss business. These lunches were very relaxed and enjoyable, but provided me with the best information as to where to find the next line. We started to deal with a range of novelty goods. We sold toys, figurines and cosmetics.

Some lines came and went relatively quickly, and I was always travelling and looking for new ideas in stores all over the world. For example, in the 1970s, I was on holiday with Freda in Canada when we spotted teenagers wearing brightly coloured toe socks that were like gloves – but for the feet! I bought a few pairs and Freda thought they would be a good line to sell. Once I was back in London, I showed the samples to the buyer for Woolworths, who expressed great interest. Two days later, I travelled to Hong Kong, where I located the manufacturer and bought a small quantity to test the market. After a brief trial of selling the product in 40 shops with great success, I ended up buying 25,000 dozen pairs of toe socks, which sold in a few weeks through Woolworths. This was an example of a fashion line that had a success for a particular time. Millions of goods were sold quickly and consequently significant profits were made. I doubt there would be a great demand for toe socks today! But this pattern of sourcing, buying competitively and selling in great quantities was repeated across a very wide range of fashion products. For instance, I had similar success when I went to Italy and bought scarves that were sold in many British chain stores.

Our strongest lines were those articles that will never go out of fashion and for which there is always a demand. At Leon Schaller and Sons, we carefully considered the British climate and the needs of our average customer and covered all possibilities. So we became the largest importer of umbrellas in the United Kingdom. I reasoned that umbrellas will always be needed in Britain! The umbrellas were produced in Taiwan and Hong Kong, and we always kept a large stock so that we could supply the shops quickly. They sold well throughout the year, but in the few warmer months when umbrellas were less in demand, we also did a major line in sunglasses and became the largest importer of sunglasses as well!

In the 1970s, we began trading in the Far East. At first, we had someone who would come from Hong Kong and source goods for us. Later, we found it was more profitable if we went to the Far East ourselves. That way, we were able to buy goods very competitively and increase our profit margin. I would travel and source goods. After this, we bought more and more from the Far East. We ordered from Hong Kong, Taiwan, Korea, Singapore and Japan. Our lines expanded hugely and included suitcases, stationery, hair accessories, mirrors, cosmetics bags, shaving sets, cameras and reading glasses.

In 1979, my son Clive joined the business, having qualified as a chartered accountant with Price Waterhouse, and I am proud of the contribution he has made to the success of the company over the years. Initially, he took up a financial role, overseeing the computerisation of our order processing and accounting systems, before turning his attention to expanding our customer base, focussing on the design and supply of cosmetics and toiletries, bath and beauty accessories, and gifts. The components for these goods were manufactured all over Europe and the Far East, packaged at our assembly plant in Hainault, Essex, and sold as customer 'own-brand' ranges to most of the major multiple retailers, supermarkets, mail order companies and department stores in the UK.

During the late 1980s and '90s the business expanded rapidly. Our warehousing and assembly plant facilities were extended, but nearly all production had moved to the Far East. During the busy seasons, we employed over 100 assembly workers in the UK and many thousands of workers in various factories throughout China, Taiwan and South Korea.

Of course the company had its ups and downs. In 1988, when Woolworths was bought out, our business went through a difficult period. But by then, thankfully, we had already begun to sell to many new outlets, including Boots, Superdrug, Lloyds Pharmacy, Bhs, Avon and Tesco. Our client base changed over the years and we even sold to Walmart, Kmart, and several other prominent retailers in the United States.

It is inevitable that in order to survive, our company had to change with the times. From my perspective, the larger the company became, the more difficult it was to be involved in every aspect of its management. So although I was delighted by the expansion of Leon Schaller and Sons Ltd, I still look back with nostalgia to the early years, when the company was like a close-knit family and I was able to establish personal relationships with buyers, built on service, loyalty and trust.

The opening of our Hong Kong office

Chana Schaller, 1947

Bernard (Berl) and Chana Schaller, 1950s

Berl Schaller with Malcolm, 1950

Berl Schaller with Malcolm dressed as a cowboy, 1953

Freda with Malcolm and Leon, 1950

Leon with Berl and Chana, Bournemouth, 1965

Malcolm, Linda and Clive, summer holiday, 1964

Family in Paris, 1964

Freda on holiday, 1964

With Clive, Freda, Malcolm and Linda before our skiing holiday, 1964

Linda on holiday in Bournemouth

Our silver wedding, 1972

Clive, Linda, Leon, Freda, Janice and Malcolm at our silver wedding

With our parents, Berl and Chana Schaller, and Golda and Jacob Zaltsman

Freda and I at home, 1970s

With Freda on the QE2, summer 1985

With my great-granddaughter, Olivia, daughter of Russell and Charlotte

Olivia swimming

Olivia's first attempt at skiing

The Freda Schaller Beth Hamidrash, Ilford

Leon with the Chief Rabbi, Lord Jonathan Sacks

The consecration of the Freda Schaller Beth Hamidrash, Ilford, 3 June 2009

DONATED BY
LEON AND FREDA SCHALLER AND FAMILY
IN HONOUR OF THE DEDICATED WORK
CARRIED OUT BY ALL DOCTORS,
NURSES AND STAFF IN THE DEPARTMENT
OF CARDIOLOGY AT MEIR GENERAL HOSPITAL

With Freda and Dr Daniel David at the Meir Hospital, Kfar Saba, 1985

ISRAEL

Because I came to London as a refugee, I have always had a feeling that I don't quite belong. Wherever I am in England, I always feel part of a minority group. Although I have led a very happy and fulfilling life here, and it is the place that I chose to live and raise my family, the insecurities from my early experiences are still with me.

Since I was born in the country where Nazism originated, like most people who have experienced persecution, I have always felt a lingering fear that having been driven out of my home once, such things could happen again.

Israel is the greatest miracle of my lifetime – to have a homeland which provides a sanctuary for Jewish refugees from all corners of the earth is a tremendous gift for our people. From my earliest visit to Israel with Freda in 1973, I felt the warm embrace of its people and immediately we had this wonderful sense of belonging, a feeling that I had never experienced until then.

When Israel was established on 14 May 1948, I was just about to begin married life and had a fledgling business business to develop. At the time, my focus was on providing a secure foundation for my wife and having a family. The early years of our marriage were concentrated on working hard in the company and on raising our children, so although we were always supportive of Zionist causes, my deeper involvement with supporting Israel only developed from the 1980s when my business was successful and our children were grown-up.

The excitement of being able to contribute something significant to a new country is incredible. For a country that has only been in existence for 60 years, to have developed so rapidly in so many areas is one of the remarkable achievements of our people.

As a family, we have been visiting Israel for over 30 years. Once, in 1985, I was feeling unwell and fainted, probably due to sunstroke and dehydration. Because we were on holiday in the area, I was admitted to the Meir Hospital in Kfar Saba.

Fortunately, my sunstroke was nothing serious and I recovered very quickly, but my admission to the hospital gave me the opportunity to see the workings of an Israeli hospital from the inside. I visited other patients and spoke to the doctors. One patient was on a very complex life-support machine. When I asked the doctors about it, they told me that these machines were very expensive; there were few of them around in Israel at the time and they had the machine on loan from a neighbouring hospital. I was very happy to be able to tell the doctor, Dr Daniel David, that it would be my pleasure to purchase a machine for the hospital.

This was the beginning of my involvement with Israeli medicine. Over the years, Freda and I provided funding for the purchase of respirators, cardiac monitors and incubators for the major Israeli hospitals. Of all the thrills in my life, nothing can compare to the news from Professor Jonathan Halevy, director of Shaare Zedek Hospital, Jerusalem, who called to tell me that the smallest baby ever born in

Israel was now making good progress due to the equipment that I had donated.

Together, Freda and I supported many projects both in England and in Israel, and the ones that gave us the greatest pleasure were those that helped people's lives. Because I was from a working-class background, the opportunity to study was never offered to me. I never even thought about going to university and getting anything beyond the most basic education. Education was a luxury and not one that people like us could afford. The norm for boys like me was to leave school at 14 and begin working life as soon as possible.

For this reason, education has always been something that we wanted to be able to offer to others. It gave me particular pleasure when I was awarded an OBE in 1998 for my services to Jewish education and the Jewish community. In our own family, we were delighted that our children had the opportunity to go to university and obtain professional qualifications. Malcolm is a specialist in oral surgery and prosthodontics, Clive is an accountant and Linda is a dentist.

My own experience showed me that in order to achieve an education, there had to be financial stability. In Israel, where National Service is compulsory, Israelis have to complete their military service before they begin university. This means that most Israelis start their further education in their early twenties. Israeli universities are expensive and students often have to work throughout their university course to support themselves. In addition to this, since they start their courses late, many students are married and have families, adding to the financial pressure.

In 1997, we were given the chance of sponsoring 150 army graduates through university. All the students that we sponsored came from families who were unable to finance them; some were refugees from Ethiopia and Russia and the scholarship afforded them the opportunity to pursue the careers of their dreams. I have wonderful letters from students who qualified in the fields of medicine, science and engineering and I feel really privileged to have been able to give them this start in life.

This particular project had added poignancy since it was dedicated to the memory of Yoni Netanyahu. Yoni, the brother of the current Prime Minister, was the young soldier killed while rescuing civilians in the raid on Entebbe. (In 1976, Israeli forces stormed a plane that had been hijacked by terrorists, rescuing the captured passengers who had been flown to Uganda.)

With Prime Minister Binyamin Netanyahu and his wife Sara, 1997

It was my idea to dedicate the scholarship to the memory of Yoni Netanyahu, since he had given his life in the service of his country. Binyamin Netanyahu was Prime Minister at the time and held a concert in honour of Freda and me. All the musicians were practising servicemen. In recognition of the award, the entire Cabinet was present at this incredibly moving occasion.

One recipient of the scholarship, who had experienced tremendous hardship, said to me,

> *I had given up on the idea that there any good people left in the world. Now that I've met you, I realise there still are some.*

Another of my ongoing interests is in building up the town of Arad. This is a new town, located in the northern Negev, east of Be'er Sheva, on a plateau 600 metres above sea level. Arad was a barren desert and has now been turned into a prosperous city. In 1962, Arad had a population of 160 residents. Today, it boasts a population of over 26,000.

When our grandson, Mark, developed asthma as a child, Freda and I became very interested in helping asthmatics and finding a cure for Mark. This led to the beginning of our involvement with the town of Arad. We first visited Arad because it was known to have very clear air, which was thought to be good for asthmatics. After establishing the first asthma clinic there, Freda and I became friendly with the mayor of Arad.

At the time, there was no centre for dealing with emergencies in Arad. Freda and I saw that there was a great need for a medical centre in the town, and with the help of our dear friend Dr David Applebaum, an expert in trauma care, we set up The Schaller Medical Centre there. Tragically, Dr Applebaum and his daughter were killed in a terrorist attack in Jerusalem in September 2003.

In Arad, as in most Israeli towns, many families depend on a dual income and virtually all the women need to go to work. Consequently, provision of good child care for pre-school children is of paramount importance. I am sure that children need the best start in life – a warm and nurturing environment is likely to promote happiness and well-being from the beginning.

In 1999, my wife and I opened the Schaller Children's Centre in Arad. This provides several new play halls, large gardens and state-of-the-art facilities so that the children of Arad can spend their early years in a secure and happy environment and in the care of a loving and dedicated staff. My hope is that the creation of this Centre will bring peace of mind and stability to hundreds of families in Arad.

Malcolm, Chief Rabbi Lord Jonathan Sacks, Leon, Linda and Clive at the opening of the Freda Schaller Beis Hamidrash, Ilford

REFLECTIONS

Looking back on my life, it divides into a few totally distinct chapters. The first was a happy and carefree early childhood in Cologne, surrounded by love and safe in the company of family and friends. This early childhood seems to be so different from my subsequent experiences and the life I was to lead from the time that I arrived in England. But I really believe that the early years of stability provided me with a great sense of security. Possibly, this firm foundation gave me the confidence and strength to face the challenges that confronted me later.

I was just a teenager when I first encountered the Nazis on the streets of our home town, but I had probably experienced antisemitism far earlier. Despite all that was negative and destructive in Germany, my parents had instilled certain values in me. They had taught me to work hard and to always try my best to help others. These values helped me get through the difficult intervening years. Even when my parents were not with me, their clear example and strong moral values guided me throughout my life.

In business and in communal life, the same principles guided me, irrespective of whether I was a delivery boy for the local butcher or the managing director of my own company. As a long-term supporter of the Conservative Party, I was a guest at 10 Downing Street on several occasions. My support and respect for Margaret Thatcher when she was elected as Prime Minister reflected our shared beliefs about personal enterprise and the economy.

Because of my involvement with the Conservative Party, I was able to use my influence to help some of the causes that were very close to my heart. I was approached by Sidney Frosh, the President of the United Synagogue, for my support in the establishment of a new Jewish secondary school in Ilford. Consequently, I visited Gillian Shephard, the Conservative Secretary for Education. As a result of this, we were able to secure the financial support that was ultimately to lead to the setting up of a new Jewish secondary school in Ilford. The King Solomon High School was established in 1993.

None of this would have been achieved without the support of my dear wife, Freda. While my parents were the main influence in my formative years, Freda became my soulmate in my adult life. She was my rock, the foundation upon which our family was built. Although we married young, we grew up together. We both loved the family life and because of Freda's secure and reassuring presence, I was able to fulfil my ambitions in business. Despite my work commitments, I always ensured that I was there for my children. When they were little, I enjoyed taking them to primary school. I often attended events like their sports days that were held in the park next to our house. Although I travelled a great deal, whenever possible I tried to be home in the evenings to kiss them goodnight. Freda was not a public figure; she was private and practical, but her wise counsel guided me. We worked on all our communal and charitable ventures together. Her passing on 20 February 2008 left me and our children broken-hearted.

I was overwhelmed when I read the personal and very moving tributes from my friends, both here and in Israel. I am so very grateful to have been in touch with so many inspirational people – politicians, doctors, rabbis and educators. It struck me that there are numerous incredible individuals, all working in their own areas in an attempt to make the world a better place.

I have been fortunate to be able to be involved in so many interesting and worthwhile projects. Many of these ventures are still ongoing and, looking around the world today, there is still plenty of work to be done and I have no intention of slowing down! Having withdrawn from the world of business, I have the wonderful opportunity to increase my involvement in the lives of my children and grandchildren. They know that working to make a difference in the lives of individuals is what provides me with the greatest pleasure.

TRIBUTES FROM FRIENDS
AND COLLEAGUES

"The best way of knowing what can be done in a single lifetime is to read such stories, for they take us beyond theory and abstraction and show us living examples of moral greatness..."

Chief Rabbi Lord Sacks

Professor Jonathan Halevy

Director Shaare Zedek Medical Center
Jerusalem
Israel

Leon Schaller has always been a man of vision, whose philanthropy has always been guided by a selfless desire to help others. It is well known that he has a great love for Israel and directs many of his philanthropic ventures to benefit our institutions. There is little doubt that this is driven by his appreciation for the centrality of Israel in the modern Jewish experience, which in large part derives from his personal experiences. Here at Shaare Zedek Medical Center in Jerusalem, the Schallers have been the supporting force enabling us to purchase much of our ultrasound equipment. That commitment now benefits thousands of our patients each year.

It is most difficult to speak of Leon without Freda as they were the ultimate partnership, as parents, as community leaders and as lovers of Israel. Last summer, together with his three children and grandchildren, Leon dedicated the Doctor's Examination and Treatment Room in the Department of Paediatric Emergency Medicine in Freda's honour. This ensures that his beloved wife's memory will always be remembered in the very same way in which she lived – in a spirit of giving and caring for the needs of others.

Freda and Leon at Shaare Zedek Medical Center

ANGELA MARGOLIS-RAZ

Director
Director of the British Council
Shaare Zedek Medical Center
London

LEON SCHALLER OBE

My acquaintance with Leon Schaller began shortly after I was appointed executive director of the British Council of the Shaare Zedek Medical Center in 1986. The Chief Rabbi and Lady Jakobovits hosted a dinner at their home in aid of the Jerusalem hospital and Leon and Freda were amongst the guests. Leon was a successful businessman, debonair and elegant, thoughtful and compassionate. I was impressed by his total commitment to Israel and his desire to do whatever he could to support its institutions.

He subsequently donated a high-frequency respirator to Shaare Zedek's Neonatal Intensive Care Department. When I told him one day about a premature baby whose life had been saved by this piece of equipment, he was intensely moved and the image of this tiny newborn has remained with him to this day. His emotional response typified his determination to make people's lives better. And if he could achieve that through improving their health and by helping Israel's development, then he was doubly satisfied.

Our friendship developed over the years, and as I learnt more about Leon's personal history and his philosophy of life, I grew to understand the motivation behind his fervent belief in Israel as the pivot of the Jewish world. He has a great thirst for knowledge and information and is always anxious to hear "what's happening" in Israel.

On one occasion, Shaare Zedek's Director-General, Professor Jonathan Halevy, and I were sitting with Leon in the lounge of a well-known London hotel, when I was called away to the telephone. Leon and Jonathan were so engrossed in their conversation that they did not even notice the man who stole my handbag, which I had left sitting, I thought, safely between the two of them, from right under their noses.

On a personal level, I enjoyed many memorable social occasions with Leon and his family. My husband and I took Leon and his dear late wife Freda z"l on several day trips when they were in Israel and we enjoyed many meals together in Israel and in London. We shared their celebrations and when Freda tragically passed away, tried to comfort Leon in his great sadness. Freda z"l was an elegant, gentle and gracious lady who has left an indelible mark on the lives of all who were privileged to know her. I remember the long telephone chats we used to have when Leon was out at meetings with the many people, whether from Israel, the UK or other places in the world, who sought his advice and support. I don't believe that many of them were disappointed.

Leon's support for Shaare Zedek Hospital has been stalwart and thousands of patients owe their health, and even their lives, to the many pieces of equipment he has donated over the years. He is affectionately known as "Mr Ultrasound" by hospital staff. I remember once sitting with Leon in his beloved flat in Israel, overlooking the Mediterranean, explaining the urgent need for a mobile x-ray machine. He promised to think about it and as I got up to leave, he said, "Don't worry, my dear, I won't let you down." And he never has.

Professor Yehuda Shoenfeld

Head of Department
Center of Autoimmune Diseases
Chaim Sheba Medical Center
Tel Hashomer
Israel

I met Leon and Freda for the first time close to ten years ago, via a family connection. As we met, a very warm electrical current crossed between us, as we belonged to the same family. I invited Leon and Freda to a short visit of our department of Medicine 'B' in the Sheba Medical Center, Tel-Hashomer (which is the largest hospital in Israel, circa 2,000 beds). The first question Leon asked me was, "How can we save more lives in this department?" And when I answered, "Having more monitors," the next week we had 8 modern monitors so that up to now hundreds of patients' lives have been saved, with the monitors alerting us to their sudden heart problems. Since then, on almost every visit of Leon and Freda to Israel (which were very frequent), Leon has found an excuse to contribute to some ideal purposes. Over the years, a significant portion of our modern equipment in the department has carried the name O.B.S. Schaller, and helped many patients and eased the work of the medical team.

Leon did not distribute his money in vain. He was always looking for a real great purpose for Israel, which will benefit a large number of subjects. This explains how he came to donate a nice sum of money to enable veteran soldiers to achieve high education upon their discharge from service. He also contributed special shoes to a combat unit (commando), so that their running, climbing and jumping on very rocky terrain will be easier and more efficient.

Leon participated in all of our celebrations and is regarded as the "father" of the department. Recently, he has embarked on high endeavour to build the new "Center for Autoimmune Diseases," a 3,000-square meter institution consisting of physicians' rooms, laboratories, day care and centre for clinical studies, to which he donated a significant amount of money.

Over the years we have had hundreds of dinners together, in which our main discussions were related to the political situation of Israel, during peace and war times. Leon showed an impressive understanding of what is going on, and even more so for what should be done. Needless to say that he met quite frequently with political figures in Israel to better understand the situation.

There is no question that the names of Leon and Freda are engraved in many institutions in Israel, but also in the ground and rocks of the country.

Freda with Yehuda Shoenfeld, Tel Hashomer, 2001

Mr Avraham Kaminer

Chairman
Arad Foundation
Israel

RE: MR LEON SCHALLER OBE AND THE ARAD
FOUNDATION

Leon Schaller began his wonderful relationship with the City of Arad
and the Arad Foundation in 1991.

A direct connection was made between Mr Schaller and Avraham
Kaminer, former Deputy Mayor of the City of Arad and Representative
of the Gur Hassidic community of Arad.

Over the years, Mr Schaller has become a very close friend and
trusted confidant of Rabbi Kaminer, who is now the Chairman of the
Arad Foundation. Mr Schaller also became a close friend of former
Mayors of Arad, Mr Bezalel Tabib and Dr Moti Brill.

Mr Schaller and his late wife Freda, of blessed memory, were the
driving force behind the establishment of the British Friends of Arad
and pushed Rabbi Kaminer to set up a "Friends" network that would
lend credibility and status to Arad among the Anglo-Jewish community,
and further afield.

The Schaller Family have indeed been staunch supporters and
champions for the city of Arad and its inhabitants. The family has been
intimately involved in the city and its development for many, many years.
Their unbridled generosity to the city and to the myriad of projects in
which they have been involved – both publicly acknowledged and those
less public – are an inspiration to Rabbi Kaminer in particular and the city
in general. Leon Schaller was a tremendous believer in taking the

necessary steps to strengthen the city and its services and, in more private conversations, Mr Schaller still expresses concern at the state of the city and the Bedouin communities surrounding the city.

Mr Schaller was the initiator and primary donor to the largest single project in the Arad Foundation's history – the Schaller Emergency Medical Centre in Arad.

During the night and over the weekend, when the doors of the city's regular medical clinics are closed, the people of Arad and the surrounding areas had been left with no proper medical service for many years. Emergency cases occurring outside of office hours had to be taken to the Soroka Medical Centre in Beersheba – a journey of 45 minutes along roads of varying quality. The journey from the Dead Sea Hotel region to Soroka Beersheba could take up to 90 minutes. With the tremendous assistance and drive of Leon Schaller, the Schaller Medical Centre was opened in Arad in 2004.

The Schaller Medical Centre now treats around 11,000 people annually, for various medical ailments and treatments. Treatments are provided to all populations in the North Eastern Negev region, including the local Arad population, neighbouring Bedouin communities and tourists frequenting the region.

As a result of the Medical Centre and for example, the efficient use of excellent digital x-ray machines and online radiography equipment, around 95 per cent of people who are actually sent to Soroka Hospital in Beersheba are admitted as in-patients.

This attests to the tremendous improvement in medical care in Arad and the efficiency, tremendous cost-savings and reductions in inconvenience that have prevented an overwhelming majority of unnecessary journeys to Beersheba.

The Schaller Emergency Medical Centre has also saved many lives since its inception, by offering advanced and rapid medical care to the

At the opening of the Children's Centre, Arad, 1999

Arad population, often stabilising patients who need more serious medical attention, before their transfer to larger medical institutions.

The Schallers also donated and dedicated a clinic for child asthmatics, together with dormitory accommodation for the clinic.

In the field of education, Mr Schaller has been a strong supporter of projects and initiatives in Arad. Leon and Freda Schaller dedicated a large kindergarten in Arad, as well as countless educational projects to the Hassidic community's Educational Campus in Arad.

In 2003, the City of Arad awarded Mr Leon Schaller OBE with the "Honorary Citizenship" of the City, in recognition of his tremendous contribution to Arad over the years.

On behalf of the people of Arad, I would like to bless Mr Schaller with a long life, good health, and that his name should be synonymous with Arad as a place of excitement, development and success, and in the name of the 27,000 residents of Arad, a heartfelt and deep debt of gratitude to Mr Schaller for all of his work, tireless efforts and appreciation for his generous contributions to our wonderful city.

The Schaller Medical Centre, Arad

MR SPENCER LEWIS

Headteacher
King Solomon High School
Redbridge
London

I am delighted to write to you in connection with the ongoing help and support our school has enjoyed from Mr Leon Schaller over the years. Since the opening of the school Mr Schaller has continuously supported the school through generous donations to our original building fund. Hundreds of young people continue to benefit from this on a daily basis as they enter the Schaller Wing to study and enjoy their learning. Mr and Mrs Schaller donated Sefer Torah to our school from which we leyn every week during shacharit. Our students are afforded a unique Jewish education through Mr Schaller's generosity, in particular through his help with our annual Poland trip which brings so many of our young people back to their Jewish roots through what they see and experience on the trip. In addition, everyone at King Solomon has nothing but enormous gratitude for Mr Schaller's hard work during the time he was a school governor. His wise counsel and eagle eye for detail were a real asset.

If only we had more people in the community like the Schallers.

Mr Maurice Shear

Chairman
Ilford Synagogue
London

LEON SCHALLER OBE

It is more than 50 years since Leon became a member of Ilford United Synagogue. Even though his contemporaries have moved from the area during that period, Leon has remained and attends the Shul as much today as he did then. He has always been passionate about our Shul and has worked, supported and represented it whenever called upon to do so.

If one looks around the Shul, the Schaller name has always been prominent for the donations that the family has given. Not only for Siddurim and Chumashim donated for family Simchas, but for the three beautiful Sifrei Torah that have been donated over the years and are still in constant use.

Recently, the Shul was honoured when the Chief Rabbi consecrated a magnificent Beth Hamedrash that Leon donated in memory of his late wife Freda. Leon not only paid the bill but designed and oversaw its build from beginning to end. This is housed in Schaller House that Leon donated many years ago and was refurbished by him not long ago. The Beth Hamedrash is in use every day and has created a beautiful atmosphere during the services it is used for.

However, not everything that Leon does for the Shul is known. For many years now, he has been subsidising any shortfall in the Shul magazine, has never refused, when asked to contribute for youth activities, and is always prepared to help to subsidise communal activities.

But it is not just money that Leon contributes. I personally, and I know many of my predecessors also, am always pleased to get his advice concerning matters relating to the Shul; his many years of communal knowledge and experience can never be replaced.

When in London, Leon rarely misses a Shabbos service and is one of the first to arrive. Long may he be able to do so.

Every Shul needs a Leon Schaller, but we in Ilford are proud to say that he is ours.

With Chief Rabbi Jakobovits at the dedication of the new classroom block of Schaller House, Ilford Synagogue, 1977

With Lord Sacks, 2010

Dr Raphael Zarum

Chief Executive
London School of Jewish Studies
London

LEON SCHALLER – A BELIEVER IN EDUCATION

After forty long years in the wilderness, the Israelites were finally ready
to enter the Promised Land. In his last days, Moses, their leader,
prepared them for life in Israel. In one dramatic episode he tells them
that as soon as they cross the Jordan river they must assemble at a
particular location in order to renew their commitment to the Torah.
Twelve specially chosen commands would be announced and all needed
to publicly accept them. The last one of these was to *"uphold the words
of this Torah, to do them"* (Deuteronomy 27:26). But how exactly do you
"uphold" the words of the Torah? The rabbis said that as well as
observing the Torah, if a person also strengthens Jewish education by
supporting students, teachers and schools, then they are "blessed"
(Leviticus Rabbah 25:1).

Leon Schaller is truly blessed for what he has done for LSJS.
Established as Jews' College in 1855, the London School of Jewish
Studies (LSJS) is now a world-class centre of Jewish learning, brimming
with students young and old. At the centre of the LSJS Campus in
Hendon stands 'Schaller House,' which was dedicated by Leon and
Freda Schaller in 1996. Schaller House contains spacious lecture rooms,
administrative offices, a Bet Midrash and a large library of Judaica and
Hebraica.

I first met Leon in 2004 when he wanted to visit LSJS to see how
things were going. From the very beginning he was concerned that

Schaller House should be utilised as much as possible. He told me that people should be able to be involved in traditional Jewish learning in a smart and welcoming environment. He made me appreciate how important it was that our students be made to feel comfortable and treated well whenever they came into the building.

We have taken Leon's advice to heart. Schaller House is now used seven days a week – hundreds of adults attend courses, sixty students study on degree programmes, fifty teachers are there to lecture or to train, and every Shabbat it is transformed into three synagogues so that people can come to pray, eat and celebrate together. Schaller House is alive with learning, thanks to Leon's commitment and enabling attitude to education.

In September 2008, President of LSJS, Chief Rabbi, the Lord Sacks, gave the annual Ellul Lecture in memory of Freda Schaller z"l in our Main Hall. I remember Leon and Freda attending this lecture every year and with her passing we wanted to honour her memory.

Leon is a deep believer in Jewish education. He has shown unwavering support for its leaders and he displays grace and warmth to all who meet him. This is why LSJS is proud to carry the name Schaller House. The profound learning that takes place within its walls is a blessing not just for him but for all of Anglo-Jewry.

Rabbi Yitchak Bialistoski

Rosh Yeshiva
Ohel Torah Institute of Rabbinical Studies
Bayit Vegan
Jerusalem
Israel

Seven years ago, we were introduced to Leon Schaller at the home of the Chief Rabbi of the United Kingdom, Chief Rabbi Lord Sacks. The event was the 70th anniversary of our organisation. Ohel Torah was established by the late Chief Rabbi of Israel, Rabbi Yitzchak Halevi Herzog z"l, and Dayan Shmuel Hillman z"l, head of the London Beth Din.

Leon and his beloved late wife Freda had just returned from a vacation, but still made time to come to this prestigious event. Leon's reputation precedes him – people know what he does for so many people, institutions and causes. He has a personal impact on everyone he meets. Leon is the epitome of dedication, generosity, reliability and loyalty – indeed a great leader and true inspiration to us all. Being at the helm of Anglo-Jewry, Leon is a unique individual with unbelievable vision, energy and enthusiasm, whose endless activities have benefited Jews all over the world. He is "a light unto the nations".

Leon's contribution has enabled us to fund a student programme which trains rabbis and educators and sends them to lead communities and to teach all over the world. Indeed, our graduates are teaching in communities as diverse as Moscow, Munich, Sao Paolo and Panama.

With Leon's help, we have set up the "Learning Promotion Unit for Youth at Risk". This programme gives an opportunity for our students to "give" by contributing an hour a day to study with vulnerable young people. This is a mutually beneficial mentoring programme and gives young people the opportunity for personal development and the chance to study in a new way in a nurturing and secure learning environment.

We are proud to be able to share a unique friendship with Leon – the continuation of a deep friendship that began when Freda was alive. He deserves enormous recognition and we wish that in the merit of his munificent deeds, he will continue to have much *Nachas*, satisfaction, and good health in the future.

Mr Vivian Bendall

MP Ilford North 1978-1997
London

I first met Leon Schaller after I became the Member of Parliament for Ilford North in 1978. We ran a Businessmen's Dinner Club that met in the House of Commons, normally twice a year, which was addressed usually by a member of the Cabinet; this was in the early days of Margaret Thatcher.

Leon became a regular member of the Dinner Club and took a great interest in its activities. During the 1980s he became Chairman of the Dinner Club and used to thoroughly enjoy introducing the speakers on those evenings. After his period as Chairman, he then became Patron of the Dinner Club and still took a very active part, always wanting to ask questions of our guest speakers.

I know that Leon had particular admiration for the then Rt. Hon. Margaret Thatcher. I particularly remember he was extremely upset when she lost the leadership of the Party. However Leon, being who he is, soon became very enthusiastic about the new Leader, the then Rt. Hon. John Major. He also became very enthusiastic and was very much involved in Ilford North Conservative Association, giving generous contributions to the Association and always happy to provide raffle prizes for events held. He was not only a generous contributor to our Association but also a generous contributor to the Central Party funds and used to attend dinners held by the Treasurers of the Party.

At our dinners in the House of Commons, he was often accompanied by his late wife, Freda, and other members of his family.

I remember once being asked by Freda to organize a secret 70th Birthday Anniversary Party which was held at the St. Stephen's Club in Queen Anne's Gate and came as a complete surprise to Leon, and proved to be a great success.

It has been a great privilege for me to have known Leon for well over 30 years and to have had the pleasure of his company and wise counsel on numerous occasions.

I remember particularly at a time when there were problems in our Association, going to see Leon at his offices in Hainault and receiving what proved to be very good advice. It is, therefore, a great pleasure to be able to contribute to this biography, to a man who has not only been generous to the Conservative Party but has been extraordinarily generous to numerous charities that he has supported throughout his life.

To use a phrase used by Leon, "God Bless."

The Pitsburgher Rebbe with Leon

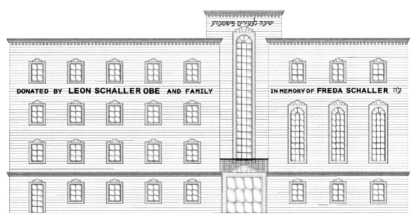

Architect's drawing of the new yeshiva, Ashdod

Rabbi M. Leiffer

The Pitsburgher Rebbe
Ashdod
Israel

The Talmud says: *There are three defining character traits by which we recognise a Jew – the attributes of mercy, modesty and the pursuit of kind deeds.* I would like to pay tribute to an exceptionally special man who exemplifies these traits.

Leon Schaller is a beacon of light, a person to emulate, a shining example of someone who can reach a high level of sensitivity and empathy. I have no words to describe my appreciation of him. Those who are privileged to know him feel enriched. I am fortunate to share a close, loving and brotherly friendship with Leon and I feel that he is part of our family.

I would like to share an example of my personal experience which exemplifies Leon's very essence. We were once together on a tour of our institutions. Leon saw that our high school students were learning in 'portacabins'. He was moved to tears that our students were receiving their education in such inadequate conditions. Consequently, he felt compelled to sponsor the building of beautiful new premises for our students.

It is my hope that it is some comfort to Leon, to his family and to us that we dedicated this building to the memory of his lovely wife, Freda. She was his partner in all his charitable endeavours.

With love, grace and blessings from the past and for the future. May Leon live with G-d's help with health and happiness and pleasure from his family. May we be privileged to bask in the light of his kindness for many years to come.

Malcolm and his wife Janice, 2002

Tributes from Family

Malcolm Schaller

I was born at the beginning of the beginning of the 1950s, a few years after the Second World War had finished. It was one of the best eras to grow up in and I certainly chose the right parents. You could not wish for better parents. A doting mother and father who only wished the best for their children and strove their hardest to achieve this, always placing the children's needs before their own.

Both sets of grandparents lived within three miles of our house and I have so many fond memories of visits when every kind of Jewish delicacy was offered to us – chopped liver, potato *kugel*, *latkas*, chicken soup, *lockshen* pudding etc., with the Billy Cotton radio show or Robin Hood on in the background on a Sunday afternoon. My father and mother both looked after their parents and made sure that they did not want for anything.

My father throughout my life has always supported me and rarely criticised me. He has always rewarded success and achievement, whether at school or at home. Whether he realised it at the time, his approach spurred all his children on to try and achieve.

He was, however, admirably able to apply punishment when needed. I remember weekend mornings noisily fighting with my brother Clive on our beds, and suddenly hearing a "madman" fly into the room, a belt in his hands, striking whoever was in his way or his path. Fortunately, I was nimble enough to avoid him and run and hide in the toilet or bathroom and keep out of his way until his temper cooled down. Clive usually was not so lucky. Happy times.

My Dad has immense ability to organise and to achieve order in both his daily life and the workplace. He does not waver or deviate. One can appreciate this in everything he does, whether eating his egg, mushrooms and tomato every day and chopping it up to just the right consistency, to saying his prayers, to dealing with buyers or politicians or charities.

I have always found it astonishing that European refugees who managed to escape the Holocaust and enter the UK not speaking English were able to build up businesses and careers and prosper. My father is a marvellous example of this. Missing out on much of his education in Nazi Germany, he was still able to thrive and create a business supplying many different types of merchandise, some manufactured in the UK and much manufactured abroad. He achieved this through sheer hard work, being competitive and by achieving in business the goal that he has always been proud of and continues to be proud of: "being respected". His motto has always been "to try and do the right thing and gain respect".

He and my Mum were adamant that their children would be educated and become professionals. They gently steered the three of us into higher education and nobody could have been prouder than they were when each of their children qualified in their respective careers.

My father's philanthropy is legendary and I am constantly amazed by what he has done to help schools, hospitals and religious establishments and people in general. Whether it is providing a desperately needed piece of hospital life-saving equipment, or helping a cantor make professional recordings of his hymn-singing prayers, my father is there to help. Recently, we attended a 50th wedding anniversary celebration in a church hall. I was astounded to see my father's name on a plaque commemorating his contribution to the hall back in the 1950s.

The Schaller Medical Clinic in Arad in Israel, providing primary care to the local population, the Schaller Nursery School in Arad, Schaller House in Beehive Lane Synagogue, Ilford, and at Jews' College – I could go on naming a great many more of his fantastic achievements and generosity. Much of this was carried out when he was running a business full-time, yet he made time to be "hands on" in helping, in many cases, to make other people's dreams come true.

Similarly, his affinity for politics, and in particular the Conservative Party, helped the Ilford North constituency greatly in the 1980s and early '90s. His admiration for Mrs Thatcher allowed him to be regularly asked to attend Downing Street and the Carlton Club for dinner. I used to chuckle when I would read about the captains of industry being invited to "think-tanks". I used to be amused to imagine the captains of industry and my father discussing the economy and the way that Great Britain should be heading.

I have had throughout my life fantastic parents – a mother and father who have always been there to help me and my brother and sister, and their grandchildren. He (with my mother) has helped so many people in so many ways, which is such a great achievement and we are all very proud of his accomplishments and the respect he has held in the community.

He is a very hard act to follow.

Clive with his wife, Jennifer

CLIVE SCHALLER

Our home was full of friends and family. That's the way Dad and Mum liked it to be. We wanted for nothing. Dad supported and encouraged us to work hard and behave well, whilst Mum dedicated herself to our every need. I had a very happy childhood.

When I was seven, Dad bought two season tickets for Spurs. I was absolutely thrilled! Together, we watched the famous Spurs double side win the Cup and the League in 1961; we continued to go to football together for many years, travelling abroad to European Cup Finals and watching England win the World Cup in 1966. On one occasion, when England played at Wembley, the England team had their pre-match lunch at the Brent Hotel in Edgware. Dad booked lunch at the Brent Hotel that same day, and I actually spoke to my hero, Jimmy Greaves!

In 1971, we travelled together around the world, visiting Moscow, Israel, Hong Kong, Japan, Hawaii and Los Angeles, partly on business, partly for leisure. Whilst in Hong Kong, we met up with some of my father's long-standing suppliers for dinner at Hugo's restaurant in the Grand Hyatt. I was struck by the congeniality and friendliness around the table that night. These were genuinely warm relationships, born not only out of mutual interest, but also out of respect.

I joined my father's business in 1979 and saw at first-hand how my father dealt fairly and respectfully with all business associates. He has a charm that he used to best effect with the buyers. He was on their wavelength and had the knack of recognising a good product, 'a winner', and presenting it to the buyers in a most efficient and organised manner.

My father handled many different products and some of the deals he pulled off were remarkable. In one 'sale or return' agreement, I calculated that we would make more money if our customer returned all the goods! "You have to bamboozle them, son, and if you don't know the answer, bluff your way through it."

Throughout the period we have been in business together and long before, my father has always been incredibly generous. From the outset, he has always given what he could to charitable causes, even when he did not have much himself. He continues to live modestly whilst giving to others.

Let me conclude by also paying tribute to my gorgeous mother, who passed away two years ago. Behind every successful man there is a woman, and Mum was always there for Dad and for us all.

She is not with us today, but her memory shines bright.

She would have been so proud of you, Dad, on the publication of this book, as I am.

Dad, you are an example to us all. Thanks for everything and in your words *"Abi Gesind."*

Freda, Leon and Linda

LINDA SCHALLER

I have very happy memories of my childhood. Dad has always been a wonderful provider for all the family and Mum was always there at home for us. Our home was always full of my friends. Everyone was made welcome and Dad's teatime sandwiches were legendary.

One of my memories of my Dad was my first day in prep school. Both my parents took me and were clearly very upset when I lay kicking and screaming on the floor, as I did not wish to go to school. As soon as they left, I got up and walked into the classroom. About half an hour later, I saw Dad at the window of my classroom waving at me. He looked really relieved to see that I was OK.

As I was growing up, Mum and Dad supported me and gave me exactly the same opportunities as my older brothers, for which I will always be grateful. Saturday mornings, whatever the weather, Dad and I walked to Shul and sat together till I was twelve.

During the weekend, Dad would then take Clive to Spurs after lunch and I remember waiting patiently for them to return so we could sit down to an enormous tea. These were happy times for all.

From quite a young age, I was aware of my Dad's generosity. I remember talking to him about the Anthony Nolan Bone Marrow Trust when I was about eleven. I told him that I thought we should donate some money to it as I'd read about it in the newspaper. Dad immediately got his cheque book out and gave me a cheque to send off. He rarely said no to someone who approached him for a donation and the donations just seemed to get larger and larger.

It makes me very proud to realise what our Dad has accomplished during his life, always supported and encouraged by our wonderful Mum.

Receiving my OBE at Buckingham Palace, with Linda, Freda and our granddaughter Shoshana

Malcolm, Janice and their three sons, Russell, Marc and Gavin

The Schaller grandchildren

My 80th birthday in 2002; from the left, Gavin, Anthony, James, Alan, Freda, Leon, Shoshana, Marc and Russell

Russell, Charlotte and Olivia

And now the grandchildren...

Russell Schaller

At age four, I had my first trip to Papa Leon's factory. I was so excited; it felt like I was visiting Willie Wonka.

I was led straight up to his office. The big oak door opened and there he was, sitting behind an enormous mahogany desk, a huge stuffed lion by his side and an incredible array of colourful umbrellas scattered all over the room.

There were bags of beads, sunglasses of all shapes and sizes, gift boxes and bath toys. I didn't know what this amazing place was, but I knew I wanted to stay as long as possible.

Then Papa Leon sat me on his knee and fed me the best smoked salmon sandwiches I had ever tasted. And when we had finished, he said I could choose anything in the room to take home with me. Of course I asked for the gigantic stuffed lion which was too big to fit in the car. After a long time pleading with Mum to strap it to the roof, I went away with an umbrella and a pair of ladies' sunglasses.

Papa Leon has been the most generous and inspiring grandfather you could ever imagine. He always seems to have good advice for every situation. In business he has always told me, "Don't worry about the competition, just worry about doing the best job you can." Advice doesn't get much better than that.

Marc and Hannah

MARC SCHALLER

Recently I went on a trip to the South of France with Papa Leon. We were attending to various bits of renovation work to his apartment in Antibes – a place that was enjoyed by him and my wonderful Nana Freda for so many years of holidays in the Côte d'Azur, and subsequently by the rest of the Schaller clan for many fantastic family vacations to follow.

After close inspection of the new shower room, freshly painted walls, and reconditioned cupboards, Papa Leon promptly called the builder over to the flat. I anticipated the builder would turn up with some documents to be signed, ask to be paid and would then leave. I couldn't have been more wrong. The builder arrived at the flat and greeted Papa Leon as if he were a long lost relative. They hugged, they joked and after half an hour or so of warm conversation, I came to realise that Papa Leon had employed and befriended the same builder for the past 40 years. There was no paper work to be signed. All arrangements were made on little more than a handshake and a warm smile.

On the trip, we visited several restaurants in Antibes, in Juan Les Pins and in Cannes and each time my grandfather was greeted by the owners and staff members if not with a hug, then with a huge smile and a story of good times, old and new. In business and pleasure, Papa Leon has always shown enormous loyalty, generosity, friendship and respect to others. And for that, he'll always be a huge inspiration. Maybe one day I too will be hugged by a builder!

GAVIN SCHALLER

Going round to Nana and Papa's house was always fun when we were growing up, and especially on Friday nights. It really was a highlight of the week, sitting down with the whole family, Papa at the head of the table, throwing bread like Frisbees.

On would come a gastronomic masterpiece by Nana, with five different main courses to suit everyone. There was veal for Dad, chicken for Marc and lamb chops for Russell, and all delicious!

After dinner, amongst the din of jokes and laughter, Papa Leon would call me up to the head of the table. He would always make time to entertain us, and arm wrestling, along with his infamous hand squeeze, was his forte. I distinctly remember thinking that when I grew up, I wanted to be as strong as my Grandpa.

The time and love Papa has always put into his family is a great inspiration to me and nothing has ever been too big for Papa to do for his family. Great childhood memories of family occasions spent at my grandparents are ones I will cherish and hope to pass on through the generations.

ALAN SCHALLER

To his friends and family, Papa is a generous man who has presence and commands respect with ease. Upon closer inspection, however, he is also a reserved man, deep within his thoughts, a realm which he keeps to himself and frequents often. There have been a few times that I have been present when he philosophises, and his advice and theorizing are wise and given with the best intentions. He is a much more sensitive and pensive man than he would let on to be.

I have many fond memories of Papa, from going away on holiday with him and the family throughout my life, to getting the keys to my first car that he so kindly bought for me. Some particularly memorable times date back to when I was very young, and the whole family would meet every Friday night at Papa's. Nana would cook an enormous and fabulous meal for all of us, and we would trade stories and discuss events of the past week. Papa never said as much as everyone else, but rather would spend more time observing and chipping in when he saw fit. This unity of family is something that I know gives him great pleasure and it shows. Many of my best memories of him are from these early days in my life. He used to sneak me and my brothers sweets after dinner. Despite my father's hawk-eyed attempts for this to stop, we always managed to get a couple.

Seeing what he has achieved in his multitude of philanthropic acts, especially in Arad, and how dearly the people who live there thank him, was a real shock to me. I was still very young, and assumed that all older people were like him. I recognised then that Papa is a special man and a good figure to have at the head of the Schallers!

I know that my brothers and I owe him so much, and I hope one day that we will be able to take his example, and be as charitable and giving to everyone around us as he is.

Freda and I with our grandchildren James, Alan and Anthony

ANTHONY SCHALLER

To describe Papa is a difficult thing; the outside world sees his smart dress, his perfectly combed-back hair, and, of course, his generosity of spirit and charitable nature. To those of us who truly know him, however, there is so much more beneath this exterior. For me, Papa is an excellent role model – I see a man who has really lived, a man who has faced adversity and survived to establish himself as a success in society, and an admired figure in the Jewish community. His perseverance and determination in business, and in life, are an inspiration.

Family unity is especially important to Papa, and I have many warm memories of the times we have all spent together – the Friday night meals, celebrating Rosh Hashanah and Passover, and the holidays that we have been on. I am extremely grateful and appreciative for all that Papa has done and continues to do for me.

I would like to finish by paying tribute to my Nana, who passed away two years ago. She is dearly missed and she would be proud to know that Papa continues to support the family as he always has done. With Papa's proud, funny and altruistic character, he will always be an excellent role model for the whole family.

SHOSHANA AMINOFF

When I was a little girl, I stayed with my grandparents quite often over the weekend. Without fail every Sunday morning, I ran into their room and jumped onto the bed. I always loved their bed as it was so high that I felt like a princess whilst lying on it. After a quick snooze cuddled up next to my Grandma, I followed my Grandpa into the bathroom for what I looked forward to most during the weekend. He sat me next to the sink, in front of the large mirror that took up the entire bathroom wall, and covered my face in shaving foam. He handed me a toy razor and I would imitate him shaving. It must have looked hilarious as I took it so seriously, just like he did.

I idolise my Grandpa as much now as I did then. I wanted to mirror everything he did and, to be honest, not much has changed now that I'm 24. He has done more good than anyone I know and loves his family in the most remarkable way. He is an inspiration and without doubt the best grandfather I could ever ask for.

Shoshana and Leon

Clive, Leon and Malcolm
Russell, Gavin and Marc

Freda and Leon with Clive, Linda and Malcolm